BONAVENTURE

Timothy J. Johnson

BONAVENTURE

Mystic of God's Word

New City Press

Published in the United States by New City Press
202 Cardinal Rd., Hyde Park, NY 12538
©1999 New City Press

The translations of Bonaventure are used with permission from the following sources with few minor adjustments:

"The Minor Life of Saint Francis" translated by Timothy Johnson in *The Founder* from *Francis of Assisi: Early Documents*, ©1999 Franciscan Institute of Saint Bonaventure University (New City Press, Hyde Park, NY)

What Manner of Man: Sermons on Christ by Saint Bonaventure, edited, translated, and introduced by Zachary Hayes, ©1974 Franciscan Herald Press, Chicago

Bringing forth Christ, the Son of God. Five Feasts of the Child Jesus. St. Bonaventure, translated, and introduced by Eric Doyle, O.F.M., ©1984 SLG Press, Oxford

"Prologue to the First Book fo Sentences," translated by Eric Doyle, O.F.M., "Prologue to the Third Book of Sentences," translated by Regis Armstrong, O.F.M. Cap., and "Prologue to the Fourth Book of Sentences," translated by Gregory Shanahan, O.F.M. in *The Cord*, 1985

Prologue to the Breviloquium, Sermon for the Fifth Sunday after Epiphany, and *Sermon for the Second Sunday before Lent* translated by Dominic Monti, O.F.M.

Sermon for Passion Sunday translated by Timothy B. Noone

A Prayer for the Seven Gifts of the Holy Spirit, and *Prologue to the Second Book of Sentences* translated by Timothy Johnson

Cover design by Nick Cianfarani

Library of Congress Cataloging-in-Publication Data:
  Bonaventure, Saint, Cardinal, ca. 1217–1274.
    [Selections. English. 1999]
    Bonaventure : mystic of God's word / [selected and edited by]
  Timothy J. Johnson.
      p. cm.
    Includes bibliographical references.
    ISBN 1-56548-122-4
    1. Theology, Doctrinal. 2. Catholic Church--Doctrines.
  3. Spiritual life--Catholic Church.   4. Catholic Church--Sermons.
  I. Johnson, Timothy J.   II. Title.
  BX4700.B68A25   1999
  230'.2--dc21   99-18775
                                                      CIP

Printed in Canada

9.95

Contents

Foreword

Solemn high distinctions between theology and spirituality are of rather recent vintage, and result in the impoverishment of both. That the first task of the theologian is to pray and study was more commonly recognized in earlier Christian centuries. Purely academic theology or religious studies, untethered from an explicit commitment to a faith shaped and sustained by regular prayer, worship, indeed contemplation, is a thoroughly modern development and would have been unrecognizable on the theological landscape of previous periods of Christian history.

We stand at a juncture. At this point in our history there is a deepening realization that whatever the merits of the historical epoch called "modern," its view of human nature, history, the world, and the God-world relation, is flawed. The promises of modernity have failed to satisfy the deepest desire of the human heart for freedom, for truth, for love. Another worldview is coming to be, a way of being and perceiving named by the very slippery term "post[-]modern." Though its contours are not yet altogether clear, in the post[-]modern worldview there is a greater recognition of the importance of relationality, of interdependence, and of the irreducible role of traditions in the quest for meaning, purpose, and value. Today there is a deeper realization that the human person is not to be defined principally as a rational animal with separate faculties of intellect and will, a composite of body and soul often at odds with one another. Rather the person is a whole, a being defined by heart, *affectus,* affectivity—the capacity to be touched and drawn into relationship and interpersonal communion with another, others, and God. These features of the post[-]modern have a deep resonance with the large sweep of history referred to loosely as "premodern," specifically the high Middle Ages and the Devout Teacher, Saint Bonaventure. What an extraordinary expression of the *coincidentia oppositorum* at the heart of the Bonaventurian synthesis that an age so vastly different from the medieval as ours should find so much in common with the vision of the Seraphic Doctor and Prince of Mystics.

This thirteenth century Franciscan friar, professor at the University of Paris, minister general of the Franciscans, cardinal and esteemed ecclesiastical adviser, played a crucial role in shaping the spirituality of the high Middle Ages. He created what is arguably the richest synthesis of Christian spirituality of the medieval age, integrating insights from the Greek East and the Latin West, specifically the thought forms of the Pseudo-Dionysius with the emerging devotion to the humanity and passion of Christ Crucified. He thereby gave direction to the spirituality of Western Christianity for centuries to come.

Bonaventure lived and wrote in an age when spirituality and speculation were not yet considered strangers and rivals. Thus he was able to articulate a speculative, systematic theology enkindled by a passion for the things of the Spirit, as well as a spiritual synthesis enlivened and strengthened by the rigors of theoretical reflection.

In Bonaventure we find a theology with heart and a spirituality with spine. His genius lies in speculative synthesis, in the construction of a spiritual *summa* that weaves together an integrated understanding of human personhood, philosophy and theology. As very few others have, Bonaventure managed to bring together a vast range of insights and a plethora of disparate elements within an organic and unified system in service of the life of the Spirit.

Bonaventure's work is altogether Trinitarian, grounded in the doctrine of the Trinity and in devotion to the person of Christ, the Incarnate Word of God. In Bonaventure, theology is mysticism, or mysticism is theology, wherein abstract philosophical speculation is balanced by richly laden biblical symbolism. Hence, Bonaventure's systematic spirituality is especially resonant with two developments in contemporary theology and spirituality: The astonishing renaissance in studies of the doctrine of the Trinity; and the centrality of the Word in any Christian theological reflection or understanding of the spiritual life

Preeminent among biblical symbols in Bonaventure is that of the Word. In *Bonaventure: Mystic of God's Word,* Timothy Johnson has selected and edited a wide range of Bonaventure's writings, all of which bespeak the centrality of Christ as the Word of God. Deeply schooled in Franciscan spirituality, specifically as it is expressed in the life and legacy of Saint Bonaventure, Professor Johnson demonstrates an abundance of insight and a knowledge of sources rare in a North American scholar. Johnson's own words in these pages are lean and spare, inviting the reader to enter into the words of the Seraphic Doctor, discerning therein the Word beneath and beyond all Bonaventure's words. Johnson thus proves himself a learned disciple of the Devout Teacher. For in these pages we have not only a carefully ordered, systematic presentation of Bonaventure's own thinking and writing but, more importantly, an invitation to participate in the mystery of the Incarnate Word of God palpably present in Bonaventure's words, precisely as the Word whose name is Love beneath and beyond all words.

Michael Downey

Introduction

The Life and Writings of Bonaventure

The medieval town of Bagnoregio lies far from the well-traveled tourist paths of central Italy. The occasional visitor finds the remnants of the town perched precariously on the summit of a hill carved away by a centuries-old earthquake. It was here in 1217 that Giovanni, later called Bonaventure of Bagnoregio, was born to Giovanni of Fidanza, most probably a physician by profession, and his wife, Maria di Ritello.

Few historical records remain which would serve to document the early years of Bonaventure's life in Bagnoregio. One incident that stands out is related in the conclusion of *The Minor Life of Saint Francis* where he recounts to his fellow friars the reasons he agreed to write a biography of the saint. As a young boy, Bonaventure was near death until his mother made a vow to Saint Francis and prayed for his intercession. Once healed of his sickness, Bonaventure's life would be linked to that of the Poor Man of Assisi:

> Because of him innumerable benefits from God do not cease to abound in different parts of the world, as even I myself who wrote the above have experienced in my own life. When I was just a child and very seriously ill, my mother made a vow on my behalf to the blessed Father Francis. I was snatched from the very jaws of death and restored to the vigor of a healthy life. Since I hold this vividly in my memory, I now publicly proclaim it as true, lest keeping silent about such a benefit I would be

accused of being ungrateful. Accept, therefore, blessed Father, my thanks however meager and unequal to your merits and benefits. As you accept our desires, also excuse our faults in virtue of our prayer, so that you may both rescue those faithfully devoted to you from present evils and lead them to everlasting blessings.[1]

The University Years

The outlines of Bonaventure's life come into clearer relief around the year 1235 when he arrives in Paris to study for a master's degree in arts at the University of Paris. In Bonaventure's day Paris, not Rome, was the intellectual center of Christendom. Students from all over Europe streamed into the city on the Seine where they studied with the great masters of the University such as Alexander of Hales. Beginning with the arts, that is, logic, mathematics, physics, metaphysics and ethics, students prepared themselves for later study in the areas of canon law, medicine, or theology.

Although he may have studied earlier at the school of the friars in Bagnoregio, Bonaventure was not yet a member of the Franciscan Order while he studied the arts. The school of the friars in Paris focused exclusively on theology.[2] When Bonaventure finished his master's degree around 1243, he entered the Paris novitiate of the Franciscans. The beginning of the novitiate coincided with Bonaventure's first year of theological studies. Alexander of Hales, who himself had entered the Franciscan Order in 1236, became the prime mentor for the young theologian. Under the guidance of Alexander and another great Franciscan master, John of La Rochelle, Bonaventure took up the study of the sacred scripture. This first phase of theological studies lasted five years and culmi-

---

1. *Minor Life,* lesson 8 (VIII, 579a) found in *Doctoris Seraphici S. Bonaventurae Opera Omnia.* ed. PP. Collegii a S. Bonaventura. 10 vols. (Quarracchi: Collegium S. Bonaventurae, 1882-1902). All translations from the Latin are taken from the critical editions of Bonaventure's writings.
2. Francesco Covino, *Bonaventura da Bagnoregio: francescano e pensatore* (Bari: Dedaldo Libri, 1980) 112.

nated in his selection as a bachelor of Sacred Scripture. Two years of mandatory lecturing on selected biblical texts followed in which Bonaventure began to formulate his rich commentaries on Ecclesiastes, the Gospel of John, and the Gospel of Luke. During his initial biblical studies, both Alexander of Hales and John of La Rochelle passed away. Other Franciscan masters such as Odo Rigaldi and William of Middleton accompanied Bonaventure as he continued his studies and moved toward becoming a bachelor of sentences.

The presence of Alexander of Hales could be sensed, no doubt, in 1250 when Bonaventure began his exposition on *The Commentary on the Sentences of Peter Lombard.* This work was a compilation of Latin and Greek sources which served as a textbook for theologians. It was Alexander of Hales himself who introduced, to the objection of friars such as Roger Bacon in Oxford, Peter Lombard's collection of texts into the curriculum of the Parisian friars. In the course of two years Bonaventure produced the beginnings of his own *Commentary on the Sentences,* which in four volumes reveal the broad foundations of his keen theological insights and the initial trajectory of its future development.

The year 1252 brought the official recognition of Bonaventure as a mature theologian capable of participating in the theological disputations of the master theologians of the University. In 1254 he received the license to teach theology and was named master of the Franciscan school in Paris. As master, he now directed a series of disputations among his students on a wide variety of theological themes. A number of important works such as *The Disputed Questions on the Knowledge of Christ, The Disputed Questions on the Trinity,* and *The Disputed Questions on Evangelical Perfection* originated during this period of intense academic activity.

While each one of the preceding works reveals the penetrating characteristics of Bonaventure's theological acumen, it is the third, *The Disputed Questions on Evangelical Perfection,* that best illuminates the harsh political climate in which he taught. Similar to other masters, Bonaventure found himself embroiled in the ongoing controversy between the secular masters at the University of Paris and the new mendicant communities. The arrival of the Franciscans and Dominicans on the Parisian scene had infused the university environment with new enthusiasm but had also severely shaken the preexisting academic status quo. Although the university chancellor had conferred upon Bonaventure the license to teach theology in 1254, his secular colleagues refused to recognize him as the master of the Franciscan school. One of the secular masters, William of Saint-Amour, bitterly contested the basic principle of the mendicant orders when he wrote that the poverty practiced by the Franciscans and Dominicans was against the teaching and example of Christ. Bonaventure responded to this and other attacks with *The Disputed Questions on Poverty*. So widespread was the tension between the opposing groups that papal intervention was deemed necessary. In the autumn of 1256, Alexander IV urged the Paris masters to incorporate Bonaventure together with the Dominican, Thomas Aquinas, into the ranks of the university community. This wish was realized in August of 1257 when the two mendicant doctors were installed as masters by their associates. Bonaventure marked the occasion with a salient sermon, aptly entitled, *Christ, the One Teacher of All.*

Minister General of the Franciscan Order

Bonaventure's regency as master at the University of Paris came to an abrupt halt several months before his formal recognition when he was elected Minister General of the Franciscan Order in February, 1257. Leaving his position at the university, Bonaventure once again found himself in the middle of a political, as well as spiritual, controversy. His election took place in the midst of a tremendous, albeit contested, transformation of his community. Although Francis, the Poor Man of Assisi, was still the prevailing archetype for fraternal life, the relentless pastoral demands of the Church and a steady influx of learned clerics had altered the face of the Franciscan Order permanently. Gathered often in urban areas in large dwellings, the majority of friars now followed a stable lifestyle, which fostered learning and preaching. Many friars who still remembered the early years of the nascent community wished to remain poor, itinerant preachers and hermits. They had placed their hopes in John of Parma, whose ministry as general ended under a cloud of suspicion with the election of Bonaventure.

What provoked suspicion of John of Parma was the accusation, raised by some ecclesial authorities, of his willingness to promote certain tenets of Joachite thought. Joachim of Fiore, an abbot from Calabria in southern Italy, had spoken a century earlier of a coming age of the Spirit, which would supersede the age of the Son and lead to the elimination of the institutional Church. His millennial vision provided a fitting framework of interpretation for some friars, who conceived of Francis of Assisi and his primitive community as the harbingers of the new age. One friar, Gerardo of Borgo San Donnino, promulgated this view in 1254. He was condemned roundly by William of Saint-Amour and the other Parisian masters, who accused the Franciscan and Dominican Orders of distorting the evangelical life. In the ensuing controversy, John of Parma, whose writings contained hints of Joachite influence, resigned as Minister General. When asked who would best take up the mantle of leadership in the future, he suggested the Parisian professor, Brother Bonaventure of Bagnoregio.

While professor, Bonaventure had hinted already at his vision of the genesis and future direction of the Franciscan Order in a brief autobiographical aside found in *The Letter to an Unknown Master.* He described how his vocation as a friar was tied to his love of Saint Francis' evangelical lifestyle and the dynamic evolution of the fraternity:

> Do not be disturbed that the friars were simple and illiterate men in the beginning; this should confirm your faith in the Order even more. I confess before God that it is this that made me love the life of blessed Francis above all, because it is similar in its beginning and perfection to that of the Church, which began with simple fishermen and grew to include the most illustrious and

learned doctors. And so you will see in the Order of blessed Francis, as God displays, that it was not invented by human discretion but Christ.[3]

While the origin of the Order was revealed in the divine inspiration of Francis and other simple men like him, there was no doubt in Bonaventure's mind that the future belonged to the educated friars as well. Certainly every friar, simple or learned, could lay claim to a place within the fraternity. There would be no return, however, to what some considered to be the pristine past of Francis and his early companions.

The rapid expansion of the Franciscan Order and the indiscriminate acceptance of novitiate candidates led to numerous scandals, which Bonaventure, like his predecessor John of Parma, strove to curtail. In his *First Encyclical Letter,* written on his assumption of office in 1257, he outlined and condemned a number of abuses which had crept into the fraternity and urged the friars to return to the basic principles of Franciscan life. His *Second Encyclical Letter,* written in even harsher tones after ten years of ministry to the friars, went so far as to call for the incarceration and expulsion of those who publicly tarnished the image of the Order.

Although Bonaventure did not hesitate to threaten the lax with juridical sanctions, he preferred to motivate them and their faithful brothers by appealing to the image of Saint Francis. During his years as Minister General, Bonaventure turned repeatedly to the Poor Man of Assisi as the archetype for fraternal imitation and integration. Two years after his election, Bonaventure ascended the rugged slopes of Mount Alverna in central Italy to search, as Francis had done before him, for a taste of divine presence. It was here that Francis received the stigmata, the wounds of Christ in the heights of ecstasy. Bonaventure recognized in this experience, as he recounts in *The Journey of the Soul into God,* a form of contemplative prayer others like himself could practice. His efforts to encourage the imitation of Francis are also clearly visible in various sermons and the hagiographical

---

3. *Disputed Questions,* n. 13 (VIII, 336a-b).

account of the saint, which he authored at the request of the friars gathered in Narbonne in 1260. *The Major Life of Saint Francis,* together with the liturgical version, *The Minor Life of Saint Francis,* offers an image of the saint as a living example to all the friars, regardless of their circumstances, of what it means to live in conformity with Christ.

The task of guiding these friars fell to Bonaventure at a moment when the Order counted some thirty thousand members scattered throughout Europe. In their missionary zeal, the friars had even reached distant points in Asia and Africa. In the ensuing years Bonaventure took to the roads to meet them. His itinerary must have been as exhausting as it was exhaustive. On numerous occasions he visited Italy and France. Spain, Germany and perhaps England also welcomed him. The geography of these travels is evidenced in the chronology of the many sermons he preached to the friars, clergy, and laity of the towns where the friars had founded communities. In addition to his preaching, Bonaventure also found the time and opportunity to compose various spiritual treatises for a wide audience. *On the Perfection of Life to Sisters,* addressed around 1260 to Isabella, the founder of a Poor Clare community and sister of King Louis of France, succinctly outlined the foundations of religious life as Bonaventure understood them. *The Triple Way, The Tree of Life,* and *The Five Feasts of the Child Jesus* also date to this period of time when Bonaventure was crisscrossing Europe.

The magnitude of Bonaventure's journeys comes into perspective when we take into consideration the reality of medieval travel. Although the combination of ancient Roman roads, more modern public roads, and ferry services offered him a ready combination of travel options, it still would have taken him roughly two months to journey from Paris to his home in Bagnoregio.[4] Immersed as Bonaventure was in the pastoral responsibilities of his office, he nevertheless returned to the University of Paris when circumstances such as a re-

---

4. Jacques Bougerol, *Introduzione generale alle opere di san bonaventura* (Roma: Città Nuova Editrice, 1990) 20-22.

newed attack on the mendicants or the controversial use of Aristotelian thought warranted his presence. Two works, *The Defense of the Mendicants* and *The Collations on the Six Days,* dating from around 1269 and 1273 respectively, reflect his thoughtful response to these challenges.

The last challenge Bonaventure faced was the organization of the Second Council of Lyons. Named a cardinal by Pope Gregory X in 1273, he was called upon to assist him in the conciliar preparations. Among other accomplishments, Bonaventure proved to be instrumental in laying the groundwork for reconciliation, albeit brief, between Rome and the Greek Churches. He died during the council, on July 15, 1274. A papal chronicler captured the atmosphere of the moment and the enduring legacy of Bonaventure:

> Brother Bonaventure of glorious memory, cardinal bishop of Albano, died at the end of the fourth session of the Council of Lyon . . . at one in the morning during the night between July 14 and 15. He was a man of knowledge and distinguished eloquence, illustrious in holiness, life, conduct and customs. Loved by God and people, he was good, affable, pious, merciful, and full of virtue. He was buried that Sunday in the church of the Friars Minor of Lyons. The Lord Pope was present at the rites together with all the cardinals, almost all the prelates of the Council, and the entire curia. The Dominican friar, Pietro di Tarantasia, formerly the archbishop of Lyons and now the cardinal bishop of Ostia, celebrated the mass and preached on the theme from the Second Book of Kings: *I cry for you, my brother Jonathan* [1:26]. There were many tears and anguished sighs. God had given him, in fact, such a singular grace that whoever met him was moved by a heartfelt love for him.[5]

Despite the obvious affection of many, both inside and outside the fraternity, Bonaventure remained a controversial fig-

---

5. The Latin text is found in Jacques Bougerol, *Introduzione generale alle opere di san bonaventura*, 14, note 20.

ure for those brothers who saw his administrative attempts at mediating and unifying the various factions of the Franciscan Order as a renunciation of the primitive ideal of Saint Francis. Perhaps for this reason, he was not canonized until April 14, 1482 by Pope Sixtus IV.[6] Any possible opposition notwithstanding, Bonaventure's enormous influence on the articulation and development of Christian spirituality is testified to by the innumerable copies of his works which were studied, meditated upon, and passed on to succeeding generations of grateful readers, Franciscan and otherwise. Bonaventure's intense desire for union with God, which permeates his writings, impelled Pope Sixtus V to declare him a Doctor of the Church with the title "Doctor Seraphicus" on March 14, 1588.

The Word of God and the Spirituality of Bonaventure

As a young friar, Bonaventure was fascinated by the spiritual insights of the Gospel of John into the dynamics of the Christian life. The reflections found in his early commentary of that work, which focuses on Christ as the Word of God, continued throughout his life. His spiritual treatises, scholarly disputations, theological commentaries, and homilies evidence an abiding interest in the central position of Christ in the life of every Christian and the ever-present call to union with the Word of God.

It is Bonaventure's consuming desire for union with God which marks him as a mystical author. Like so many of the eminent spiritual writers who preceded him in the Christian East and West, Bonaventure displayed a natural reticence when describing what contemporary authors characterize as spiritual experience. The paucity of autobiographical references to his interior life does neither disqualify him from inclusion among the great mystical writers of the Christian tradition nor imply he lacked those experiences characterized as mystical. The medieval world of his day and, in particular, the theological mi-

---

6. André Vauchez, *Ordini mendicanti e società italiana XIII-XV secolo*. Trans. Michele Sampaolo (Milano: il Saggiatore, 1990) 268-269.

lieu in which Bonaventure lived and worked, applied a different set of criteria when reflecting upon and defining the dynamics of spirituality. Perhaps the title of his popular work, *The Journey of the Soul into God,* best summarizes the medieval perception of the spiritual life. For Bonaventure, the appeal to personal experience was not nearly as significant as the need to integrate the various dimensions of the Christian tradition into a synthesis of life faithful to the gospel and responsive to the spiritual needs of his contemporaries. He was convinced that this expression of evangelical life, prefigured in Francis of Assisi and lived out in the eternal mystery of God's Word, fostered the transformation of individuals, communities, and, ultimately, the entire cosmos in Christ.

The Professor as Mystic

The initial outlines of Bonaventure's spirituality are evident in his exploration into the mystery of Christ found in *The Commentary on the Gospel of John.* This early text, together with his other university writings, gradually took form as he invited his Parisian students to consider Christ, the Second Person of the Trinity, as the Word of God. In the midst of classroom disputation, mirrored in the queries and responses of *The Commentary on the Gospel of John,* the question arose as to why the evangelist John chose the title of "Word." The common assumption was that he should have selected instead a seemingly more popular title such as "Son" when speaking of the only begotten of the Father.

Bonaventure's response to this question reflects his own intellectual predisposition. As a convincing writer, teacher, and preacher, the richness of the concept "word" was not lost on him. He notes in *The Commentary on the Gospel of John* that the title "Son" is of limited use in describing Christ, because it refers exclusively to his relationship with the Father.[7] The title "Word," rooted in the rich etymology of "word," has numer-

---

7. *Commentary on the Gospel of John,* c. 1, resp. (VI, 247b).

ous nuances, which illuminate the multiplicity of relation-
ships proper to the Son of God. This is because the term
"word," to a medieval mind such as Bonaventure's, referred to
the one who pronounces the word in question, what is said
through that word, the sounds that envelop the word, and the
effect on another of what is said by the word. According to
Bonaventure, the title "Word" is a far more appropriate desig-
nation for Christ, because it encompasses his relationship as
the Word of God with the Father, the myriad creatures created
through the utterance of the Word, the flesh of humanity
which clothed the Word in the incarnation, and the eternal
truths the Word proclaimed to the world.

With his response to an apparent theoretical question concerning a christological title, Bonaventure provided his students with a profound insight into the nature of Christ and a
firm foundation for a spirituality marked by a desire for, and
response to, the Word of God wherever revealed. This unique
Word of God is encountered especially in the contemplative
reading of the Book of Creation and the Book of the Scriptures. Books were understood in medieval culture as remind-
ers, in the Platonic sense, of knowledge once possessed. The
book metaphor was used to illuminate the process of learning
or re-learning.[8] The Book of Creation, which comprises countless creatures throughout the cosmos, was created through
Christ, the uncreated Word of God. These creatures, each one
a word of God in its own right, narrate the divine mystery by
recounting the creative presence of God evident everywhere.
Similar to other books, the Book of Scripture also serves to re-
mind readers of what they once knew. In this case,
Bonaventure holds that the Book of Scripture, which relates
the story of salvation in Christ, the incarnate Word of God,
was provided through the mercy of God. According to *The Disputed Questions on the Trinity,* this providential action was necessary as human transgression had obscured the signs of the

---

8. *Commentary on the Gospel of John,* c. 10, n. 33 (VII, 263b).

divine presence originally evident in the Book of Creation.[9]

From Bonaventure's perspective then, right reading, that is, contemplative reading, is the spiritual hallmark of those desiring to know Christ. As *The Commentary on the Gospel of Luke* suggests, contemplative reading entails a discerning rumination of the physical world as creatures everywhere proclaim the eternal, uncreated Word of God through whom they came into being. Likewise, contemplation requires the close scrutiny of sacred texts, as the events of salvation history manifest the presence of the incarnate Word through whom the cosmos was reconciled to the Father.[10] Another university work, *Christ, The One Teacher of All,* notes that knowledge of God's Word as uncreated and incarnate, however garnered, is to be understood in light of Christ as teacher. Marking his installation as master of theology, Bonaventure encourages those present to consider the true master of contemplative knowledge, Christ the teacher. Alone among masters, Christ directs the search for knowledge, removes obstacles to it along the pathway, and brings it to fulfillment in the bestowal of divine wisdom. This wisdom, the greatest of all spiritual gifts, brings about ultimate transformation and union with Christ.

The Administrator as Mystic

Duly installed as master of theology, Bonaventure could not, however, take on the incumbent responsibilities. As the newly chosen Minster General of the Franciscan Order, his time and energy would be directed elsewhere. On election as Minister General, the focus of his theological reflection began to shift from the university classroom to the chapter or community meetings room where the friars considered, debated, codified, and enfleshed the principles of Franciscan life. While he was no doubt ever eager to return to the Paris environs, Bonaventure began the arduous work of administration proper to his new office by traveling throughout Europe. On the road he pondered

---

9. *Disputed Questions on the Trinity,* q. 1, a. 2, resp. (V, 54b-55a).
10. *Commentary on the Gospel of Luke,* c. 18, n. 16 (VII, 470b-47 1a).

the mystery of Christ, the Word of God, Francis' spiritual experience, and the nature of the spiritual life in the context of the various pastoral needs he encountered.

A strong accent on Christ as the incarnate Word emerged early on in Bonaventure's itinerant ministry. His predilection in meditation for the humanity of Christ appears in a number of sermons and spiritual treatises composed during this period. Perhaps the two best examples of this aspect of Bonaventure's spirituality are *The Tree of Life* and *The Five Feasts of the Child Jesus*. While the theology underlining them is identical with that elaborated earlier in Paris, the tenor of the texts is remarkably different. With their appeal to the devotional affections of the reader, they utilized a genre popularized at least a century earlier by a German Benedictine, Ekbert of Schönau. Both works allowed Bonaventure to promote his insights into the spiritual life beyond the circle of people he met while traveling. They invited contemplation through the thoughtful consideration of the historical revelation of the incarnate Word. Such an attempt proffered, as *The Five Feasts of the Child Jesus* suggests, wonderful possibilities:

> In God's Church there are holy men and women who have been enlightened more profoundly than others by the divine radiance and inflamed more ardently by inspiration from on high. It is their conviction and teaching that through meditation upon Jesus and reverent contemplation of the incarnate Word, a faithful soul can experience a delight far sweeter, a pleasure more thrilling, and a consolation more perfect than from honey and fragrant perfumes.[11]

As he recounts, it was the historical events surrounding the child Jesus which attracted Bonaventure's attention at this time. He extended his contemplative gaze in *The Tree of Life* to encompass the broad spectrum of events comprising the life, death, and resurrection of Christ. Whereas *The Five Feasts of the*

---

11. *Five Feasts of the Child Jesus*, prol. (V, 88a).

Child Jesus promotes the spiritual conception of the Word in the soul dedicated to God, *The Tree of Life* speaks of the union between disciple and the crucified Christ.

Bonaventure returned repeatedly to the question of discipleship and contemplation during his travels as Minister General. Perhaps it was the struggle of many to follow Francis' example of evangelical living that elicited his ever-growing interest in the practical expression of contemplation. He explicitly addressed this fundamental dynamic in *The Rule for Novices* and *On the Perfection of Life for Sisters.* Although the needs of each group were different, given their relative degrees of spiritual maturity, the christological matrix of contemplation was crucial for both religious communities.

Quite conscious that some had abandoned prayer, Bonaventure was convinced that friars, who promised to walk in the footsteps of Jesus Christ, needed to place the incarnate Word at the center of their contemplation from their moment of entrance into the Franciscan Order. As novices, it was necessary to learn the first steps along the contemplative path through their devout recitation of the psalms. Learning to bring the sentiments of heart into harmony with the words of scripture, the novices could enter into union with Christ, who suffered the most painful of deaths for love for them. For their part, Isabella and the sisters of Longchamp certainly required no reminder as to the crucial role of the psalms for those wishing to embrace a cloistered, contemplative life. Instead, Bonaventure responded to her request for direction by holding up the crucified Christ as the beloved spouse of the sisters. A relationship with him, when nurtured in silence and prayer, would culminate in the union of mystical betrothal. Like wax to the flame, the sisters' hearts would melt in ecstasy, embraced in transforming love of the Crucified.

The theme of the incarnate Word as the crucified Christ, ever present during Bonaventure's administrative years, takes on particular prominence in *The Journey of the Soul into God.* Wearied, no doubt, by the incessant demands of ministry and anxious for consolation, he retreated to the cliffs of Mount La Verna, where Francis of Assisi was sealed some years earlier with the wounds of Christ. In a rare autobiographical note, Bonaventure recounts his longing for the peace proclaimed by Francis:

> Following the example of the most blessed Father Francis, I was seeking this peace with panting spirit—I a sinner, who, completely unworthy, was the seventh Minister General of the Friars after his death. It happened about thirty-three years after the Saint's death that I, beckoned by the divine, withdrew to Mount La Verna, a place of quiet where, with loving desire, I might search for peace of spirit. While staying there, I was considering the various ways the soul ascends into God. Among other things, the miracle that had occurred in this same place to blessed Francis came to mind: the vision of a Seraph raised up like the Crucified. As I was considering this, I saw immediately that the vision represented the ecstasy of Father Francis in contemplation and the way which leads to it.[12]

The image of the crucified Christ, together with that of the Seraph, serves as a deftly woven thread running throughout Bonaventure's reflections on Francis' spiritual experience on Mount La Verna. Before outlining the six ways of contemplation symbolized by the wings of the Seraph, readers are reminded that the path they intend to embark upon is entered through the purifying love of the crucified Christ. There is no other way, as the Crucified alone cleanses any transgressions which might obstruct prayer. Once opened to the outpouring of grace, the perception of the divine presence mirrored in the Book of Creation is possible. As the mind is raised in admiration of the wonders of the world, the image of the Seraph stands in the background as a reminder of the love of the crucified Christ, which lifted Francis into the mystery of God. This dynamic continues throughout, as Bonaventure moves beyond the world to the consideration of two specific attributes of God spoken of in the Book of Scrip-

---

12. *Journey of the Soul into God*, prol., n. 2 (V, 295a-b).

ture: being and goodness. The culmination of the ascent into God is found, paradoxically, in the crucified Christ, for it is the recognition of these attributes which directs the contemplative gaze to the revelation of the divine in Jesus Christ. Here in *The Journey of the Soul into God,* as in several other works, Bonaventure sees the crucified Christ standing at the juncture of cosmic history and personal experience as the way back to the Father. The manifestation of the Father's love in the incarnate Word, the Crucified, thus becomes the enduring symbol of human transformation and union with God.

Questions concerning contemplation, the Word of God, and the significance of Francis of Assisi converged at the University of Paris shortly before Bonaventure's death. At issue among the masters was the proper use of philosophy and the nature of Christian wisdom. The challenge to the traditional relationship between the two provided Bonaventure with the opportunity to develop further a spirituality of God's Word rooted in the theological insights he had cultivated years ago as a young friar. Returning to Paris in 1273 to address a university audience in a series of evening lectures entitled *The Collations on the Six Days,* he contests the view that philosophy could supplant theology. He reiterates his conviction that the search for wisdom begins and ends in union with Christ, the Word of God. Ever the Parisian master, Bonaventure presents a compelling synthesis of Christian spirituality against the backdrop of salvation history. The contemplation of God's Word, witnessed in the ecstatic experience of Francis of Assisi on Mount La Verna, is where wisdom is to be found. In language reminiscent of earlier works, yet informed and nuanced by years of reflection and ministry, Bonaventure compares the Poor Man of Assisi to the sixth angel of the Apocalypse; he is a precursor of a new age in human history marked by contemplative wisdom, not speculative philosophy.

The Collations on the Six Days focuses on the threefold Word of God as the proclamation of the Word of the Father in eternity and time. As the eternal Word, Christ is the divine utterance through whom all of creation comes into being; as the

incarnate Word, the historical manifestation of divine compassion; and as the inspired Word, the ongoing revelation of
divine truth encountered in contemplation. The inspired
Word fosters the subjective recognition and acceptance of the
Word of God, which otherwise would remain beyond the
realm of human understanding:

> The third key [to contemplation] is the knowledge of
> the inspired Word through whom all things are re-
> vealed; indeed there can be no revelation except
> through the inspired Word.[13]

This exposition of Christ as the inspired Word signals the full
maturation of Bonaventure's insights into the Second Person of
the Trinity. Although mentioned as early as *The Breviloquium* the
inspired Word emerges as a salient spiritual theme only at the
culmination of Bonaventure's life-long reflection on the mystery
of God and the character of Christian holiness. His acknowledg-
ment of the crucial role of the inspired Word in relation to contemplation underscores the dynamic nature of following the
crucified Christ in the context of everyday life. The objective
knowledge of the eternal and incarnate Word runs the risk of remaining abstract without the continual assistance of the inspired Word. According to Bonaventure, the journey back to
God begins here, at the crossroads of divine revelation and personal response, where the Word of God, uttered by the Father, is
disclosed in the fullness of truth and manifested in those transformed by the embrace of the crucified Christ.

Texts and Translations

The frequently quoted Italian phrase, *traduttori son traditori*
or "translators are traitors," once again comes to mind as the
translations of this volume are reviewed. Despite the best of
intentions and linguistic preparation, every translator recognizes that he or she is ultimately something of a traitor in the

---

13. *Collations on the Six Days*, coll. 3, n. 22 (V, 347a).

attempt to render the meaning of the text into another language. This anthology of Bonaventure's writings confirms such suspicions while validating the efforts of the translators. The willingness to undertake the inherent risks of translation and subsequent editing underscores the desire of the translators to enter into a dialogue with Bonaventure who, as a spiritual master of the past, continues to offer direction for contemporary men and women.

Bonaventure's writings cannot be reduced to simple genius, random chance, or singular inspiration. They are linked intimately to the communities of men and women, religious and lay, whose search for meaning afforded him the opportunity to interpret the world for them. These communities served as the matrix for Bonaventure's spiritual journey and confirmed his attempts to articulate the reality of a life lived in God's presence. Although they have undergone profound changes through the centuries, these communities continue the quest for meaning while cultivating a renewed appreciation of their spiritual heritage. For this reason it was a privilege to translate a selection of Bonaventure's writings and edit others in the company of those who share an abiding interest in exploring that vision of life often summed up in the word "Franciscan." Just as Bonaventure's life cannot be understood without reference to Francis of Assisi and those who nurtured, challenged and inspired him, so, too, this volume is best appreciated as the interpretive endeavor of those sharing a bond with the worldwide Franciscan community. The translations of this volume give voice to many who still discover countless spiritual insights by ruminating on the writings of this great follower of Francis; namely, Bonaventure of Bagnoregio.

Acknowledgments

A tremendous debt of thanks is due to all who provided translations for this anthology and who waited patiently for its appearance. Patrick Markey from New City Press offered calm encouragement throughout the writing and publication process. Dominic Monti, and Timothy Noone contributed original translations that appear here for the first time in English. The translations of other Bonaventurian writings by Regis Armstrong, Eric Doyle, Zachary Hayes, and Gregory Shanahan are presented through the kindness of their publishers. Michael Downey's willingness to write the foreword is another example of his generous spirit. Thanks goes to Ingrid Peterson who critiqued sections of this work and serves still as a mentor in the essence of all things Franciscan. Marilyn Finnerty deserves high praise for her tireless editing efforts from inception to publication. It is Agnieszka, however, to whom the greatest debt of gratitude is due. Her seemingly limitless ability to enflesh the Word of God in the ordinariness of daily life confirms my belief in miracles.

The Scriptures and God's Word

The study of sacred scripture held a central position in Bonaventure's life—both as a friar and as a theologian. Francis of Assisi's commitment to the evangelical life and genuine admiration for those who mediated the richness of God's word provided inspiration for the reflections presented in this chapter. They come from the prologue of the *Breviloquium*. As the Latin title suggests, this work, from around 1257, is a "brief discourse" on theology and the essential doctrines of Christianity. For theologians like Bonaventure, the study of theology was identified closely with the study of sacred scripture. The exigencies of theological study, therefore, motivated him to unfold the mysteries of biblical revelation for his young students who, overwhelmed by the apparent obscurity of the Old and New Testament authors, sought guidance in interpreting the texts they were required to read. Bonaventure's efforts to clarify the nature of sacred scripture are still a source of assistance, as evidenced by the references to his insights throughout the *Dogmatic Constitution on Divine Revelation* from the Second Vatican Council.

The prologue of the *Breviloquium* reminds readers, both yesterday and today, that knowledge of sacred scripture is predicated by divine revelation and marked by a dynamic relationship with Christ. Since every word comprising the biblical texts is found in Christ, the Word of God, the study of scripture requires faith in Christ and serves as a privileged avenue leading to an ever-deepening knowledge of him. The opening prayer from the Letter to the Ephesians, cited by Bonaventure at the beginning of the *Breviloquium,* introduces this understanding of sacred scripture into the context of faith and knowledge of Christ. Just as faith's knowledge is spoken of in terms of breadth, length, height, and depth, so also scripture is said to have these characteristics: It has breadth because it contains legal, historical sapiential, and prophetic books; it has length because it treats history from the time of creation to the final judgment; it has height because it encompasses the heavenly hierarchies; and it has depth because it includes literal, allegorical, moral, and mystical levels of significance. Replete with such richness and diversity of meaning, the Book of Scripture, like the Book of Creation, speaks eloquently of the Word of God.

Prologue to the Breviloquium

For this reason I bow my knees before the Father of our Lord Jesus Christ, from whom every fatherhood in heaven and on earth receives its name. I pray that, according to the riches of his glory, he may grant that you be strengthened in your inner being with power through his Spirit, and that Christ may dwell in your hearts through faith; that being rooted and grounded in love, you might be able to comprehend, with all the saints, what is the breadth and length and height and depth, and to know the love of Christ that surpasses knowledge, so that you may be filled with all the fullness of God. [Eph 3:14-19]

In these words the great doctor of the Gentiles and preacher of truth, filled with the Holy Spirit as a chosen and sanctified instrument, discloses the source, procedure, and purpose of holy scripture, which is called theology. He suggests that scripture derives its origin from an inflowing of the most blessed Trinity; that its manner of proceeding corresponds to the demands of our human capacities; and that its purpose or fruit is an abundance of overflowing happiness.

Scripture does not owe its origin to human inquiry; no, it flows from divine revelation, from *the Father of lights* [Jas 1:17], *from whom every fatherhood in heaven and on earth receives its name.* It is from him, through his Son, our Lord Jesus Christ, that the Holy Spirit flows also into us. It is through that Holy Spirit, who apportions his gifts and *allots to each one according to his will* [1 Cor 12:11] that faith is given, and it is *through faith* that *Christ dwells in our hearts.* This is the knowledge of Jesus Christ from whom the authority and understanding of all sacred scripture flows. Hence, no one can begin to comprehend it unless he or she has been infused with faith in Christ—the lamp, the door, and the very foundation of all scripture. For as regards every supernatural illumination, as long as *we are away from the Lord* [2 Cor 5:6], faith is the foundation that supports us, the lamp that directs us, and the door that lets us in. It is according to the measure of faith, furthermore, that any wisdom given us by God must be gauged, lest anyone *be more wise than it behooves to be wise, but to be wise with sober judgment, each according to the measure of faith that God has assigned* [Rom 12:3]. And so, as the apostle clearly intimates in the first part of the text with which we began, it is by means of faith that the knowledge of holy scripture is given to us according to the measure of the blessed Trinity's inflowing.

The procedure of sacred scripture—unlike the other sciences—is neither restricted according to the laws of reasoning, defining, or dividing, nor is it limited to only one aspect of the universe. Rather, it proceeds, by supernatural inspiration, to give us human wayfarers as much knowledge as we need to gain salvation. And so, in language that is sometimes literal, sometimes symbolic, as in a kind of summa, it describes the contents of the entire universe, and so covers *the breadth;* it narrates the course of history, thus comprehending *the length;* it portrays the excellence of those who will ultimately be saved, thus showing *the height;* and it depicts the misery of those who will be damned, thus plumbing *the depth,* not only of the universe, but also of the very judgments of God. In this way it describes the *breadth and length and height and depth* of the entire universe, insofar as it is expedient to have a knowledge of it for salvation. Furthermore, in the way it unfolds, scripture reflects this same fourfold pattern, which will be described below. This manner of proceeding was called for by our human capacities of understanding, for the human intellect was made to grasp many and great things in a truly magnificent way. Like a certain noble mirror, it was designed to reflect the whole complex of created reality, not only naturally but also supernaturally. Thus, the procedure of sacred scripture may be considered as fully responding to the demands of our human capabilities.

Finally, the purpose or fruit of sacred scripture is not simply any kind, but the fullness of everlasting happiness. For these are writings whose *words* are of *eternal life;* they were written, not only that we might believe, but also that we might possess that life unending in which we shall see and love and our desires will be completely satisfied. Then we shall really *know that love which surpasses knowledge* and thus be *filled with all the fullness of God.* This is the fullness to which the divine scriptures would lead us, as is truly said in the words of the apostle I have cited above. This, then, must also be the goal and the intention with which the holy scripture is studied, taught, and even heard.

That we may attain this fruit and end rightly, by the straight path of scripture itself, we must begin with prayer. That is, we must reach out in true faith to *the Father of lights,* bending the knee of our hearts, so that through his Son and in the Holy Spirit he might give us a true knowledge of Jesus Christ, and together with this knowledge, love for him. By knowing and loving Christ, by being confirmed in faith and *rooted in love,* we may be able to know *the breadth, length, height, and depth* of scripture, and through such knowledge attain the all-surpassing knowledge and measureless love which is the blessed Trinity. This is the aim of the longings of all the saints; this is the resting place and the fulfillment of all that is good and true.

Once our desires and intentions are fixed upon this end of holy scripture, once we have both believed in their Source and invoked him, it remains for us to explore their unfolding, which regards their *breadth, length, height, and depth,* following the path and order of the apostle's text. The *breadth* of scripture refers to the variety of its parts; the *length,* to its description of times and ages; the *height,* to its account of the ordered levels of hierarchies; the *depth,* to the multiplicity of its mystical senses and interpretations.

The Breadth of Holy Scripture

If we wish to behold the breadth of sacred scripture, the first thing we discover is that scripture is divided into two Testaments; namely, the Old and the New. The Old is replete with many books: legal, historical, sapiential, and prophetic. There are five books in the first group, ten in the second, five in the third, and six in the fourth, for a total of twenty-six books. Similarly, the New Testament has books corresponding to these arranged in the same fourfold division. The gospels correspond to the legal books; the Acts of the Apostles to the historical; the letters of the apostles, especially Paul, to the sapiential; and the Apocalypse, to the prophetic. Thus there is a wondrous concordance between the Old and New Testaments, not only in the consistency of meanings, but also in their fourfold division. This is what was prefigured and signified by Ezechiel, who saw the wheels of four faces and a wheel within each wheel. The Old Testament is contained in the New and the New in the Old. The legal and evangelical books have the face of a lion because of their powerful authority; the historical, the face of an ox because of their convincing strength; the sapiential, the face of a man because of their keen wisdom; the prophetic, the face of an eagle because of their penetrating vision.

Now, it is fitting that holy scripture is divided into an Old and a New Testament and not into practical and speculative branches in the manner of philosophy. This is because scripture is properly founded in that knowledge which stems from faith, which grounds and supports morality, justice, and all right living; therefore, in it there cannot be any dissociation between the knowledge of things we should believe and the knowledge of moral conduct. This is not, however, the case with philosophy, which does not only treat the truth of morals but also gives consideration to purely speculative topics. Since scripture is a knowledge moving the soul to good and withdrawing it from evil, a goal accomplished by fear and by love, it follows that scripture is divided into two Testaments which, as Augustine says, "to put it briefly, differ as fear does from love."

Now, there are four ways a person may be prompted toward good and drawn away from evil: namely, by the precepts of a most powerful authority; by the teachings of a most wise truth; by the examples and benefits of a most innocent goodness; and, finally, by a combination of these three ways. This is why the four kinds of scriptural books were handed down in both the Old and New Testaments; they correspond to these four ways. The legal books move people by the precepts of a most potent authority; the historical, by the examples of a most innocent goodness; the sapiential, by the teachings of a most prudent truth; and the prophetic, by a combination of the foregoing, which their content clearly illustrates. Hence, these latter are, as it were, a recalling of all legal and doctrinal wisdom.

Holy scripture, then, is like a vast river which continually grows in size by the addition of many tributaries as its course lengthens. Scripture first began with the legal books. Later, the streams of wisdom found in the historical books were added to it. The teachings of the most wise Solomon followed; then, those of the holy prophets. Finally, the gospel doctrine was revealed, uttered by the lips of Christ incarnate, set down in writing by the evangelists, and related by the holy apostles, together with the other testimonies, which the Holy Spirit, descending on them, taught us through them. Thus, the apostles, instructed *in all the truth* by the Spirit according to the divine promise, could give the Church of Christ the entire doctrine of saving truth and, by completing holy scripture, extend the knowledge of that truth.

The Length of Holy Scripture

Sacred scripture also possesses length, which consists of its description of the times and ages from the beginning of the world until the day of judgment. It considers the world's course through three times: the law of nature, the written law, and grace. Within these three times, it also distinguishes six ages: the first from Adam to Noah, the second from Noah to Abraham, the third from Abraham to David, the fourth from David to the Babylonian exile, the fifth from the exile to Christ, and the sixth from Christ until the end of the world. The seventh, which runs concurrently with the sixth, commences with the repose of Jesus in the tomb and lasts until the general resurrection, which marks the beginning of the eighth. Thus, scripture traverses the greatest possible length, since it begins with the origin of the world and time in the first chapter of Genesis and continues until the end of the world and time in the closing chapters of the Apocalypse.

The full compass of time, running according to a triple law—innately given, externally imposed, and infused from above—rightly passes through seven ages, comes to a close with the end of the sixth. In this way the course of the macrocosm corresponds with that of the microcosm—namely, of man, for whose sake the larger world was created.

The world's first age, when the material world was formed, the demons fell, and the angels were confirmed in good, fittingly parallels the first day of creation when light was made and separated from the darkness. The second age, when the wicked perished in the flood and the good were placed in the ark, parallels the second day when the firmament was established, separating the waters. The third age, when Abraham was called and the synagogue begun, that it might be fruitful and bring forth offspring for the worship of God, corresponds to the third day when land appeared and brought forth vegetation. The fourth age, in which the kingdom and the priesthood flourished because David expanded the worship of God, corresponds to the fourth day when the heavenly lights and the stars were formed. The fifth age, in which the exiles were scattered and spread through many nations, corresponds to the fifth day in which the production of the fishes from the waters was accomplished. The sixth age, in which Christ, the true image of God, was born in human likeness, corresponds to the sixth day in which the first man was formed. The seventh age, which is the everlasting rest of souls, corresponds to the seventh day on which God rested from all the work that he had done.

These seven ages are thus distinguished by the signs found in their beginnings, whereby they correspond to the days of the world's creation. The first age is also called infancy, for just as our infancy falls into oblivion, so all memory of this first age was drowned in the flood. The second is called childhood, because as we begin to talk at that age, correspondingly, it witnessed the separation of tongues. The third is called adolescence, because as the procreative power becomes active then, so in this age Abraham was summoned, receiving both circumcision and the promise of offspring. The fourth is called young adulthood, for just as then we are in our prime, so too in this age the synagogue flourished under the kings. The fifth is called decline, for as in our declining years one's powers diminish and beauty fades, so the exile witnessed the diminishment of the Jewish priesthood. The sixth is called old age, for just as human old age is linked with death but possesses insight and wisdom, so too this sixth age of the world ends with the day of judgment, but in it wisdom advances through the teaching of Christ.

And so the whole course of the world is shown by scripture to run in a most orderly fashion from beginning to end, like an artfully composed melody through which every mind can contemplate, by means of the succession of events, the diversity, multiplicity, and symmetry, the order, rectitude, and excellence, of the many judgments, which proceed from God's wisdom governing the universe. Just as no one can appreciate the loveliness of a song unless one's perspective embraces it as a whole, so none of us can see the beauty of the order and governance of the world without an integral view of its course. Since no mortal neither lives long enough to see all this with bodily eyes, nor can any individual foretell the future, the Holy Spirit has given us the book of sacred scripture, whose length corresponds to God's governance of the universe.

The Height of Holy Scripture

Sacred scripture, as it unfolds, also possesses a height, which consists of the description of the hierarchies in their ordered ranks. These hierarchies are the ecclesiastical, the angelic, and the divine—or, in other words, the subcelestial, the celestial, and the supercelestial. The first is described clearly, the second somewhat more indirectly, and the third more obscurely still. From its description of the ecclesiastical hierarchy, we can see that scripture is lofty, and from its description of the angelic that it is loftier still, and from its description of the divine that it is most exalted. Thus we can say with the prophet: *Such knowledge is too wonderful for me; it is so high that I cannot attain it* [Ps 139:6].

This is true enough. Since things have existence in matter, they should have existence in the soul through acquired knowledge, have existence in that soul through grace, have existence in it through glory, and have existence in the Eternal Art. Now philosophy is concerned with things as they exist in nature, or in the soul by innate or acquired knowledge, but theology, as a science based on faith and revealed by the Holy Spirit, deals with things which concern grace and glory and even eternal wisdom. Theology, therefore, subjects philosophical knowledge to itself, borrowing from the nature of things what it needs to construct a mirror for the representation of divine realities. Thus, it erects a ladder, as it were, set up on earth but whose top touches heaven. All this is done through that one hierarch, Jesus Christ, who, by reason of the human nature he assumed, is hierarch not only in the ecclesiastical hierarchy but also in the angelic hierarchy and is the middle person of that supercelestial hierarchy of the blessed Trinity. Through him, from the very height of God, the grace of unction descends not only *upon the beard,* but also even *to the skirt of his garment* [Ps 133:2]: not only upon the heavenly Jerusalem, but even to the Church militant.

There is indeed great beauty in the fabric of the world; but there is far greater beauty in the Church, adorned with the splendor of holy charisms; and greater beauty yet in that heavenly Jerusalem; but the greatest beauty of all is to be found in that supreme and most blessed Trinity.

Not only, then, do the scriptures possess a most lofty subject matter, which engages our mind and raises aloft its vision, but they themselves are also most elegant, delighting the intellect in a certain wondrous manner; thus, as they deepen this pleasure more and more, they ready us for the anagogical visions of divine marvels.

The Depth of Holy Scripture

Finally, scripture has depth, which consists in its having many mystical understandings. Besides its literal meaning, in many places it can be interpreted in three ways: allegorically, morally, and anagogically. Allegory occurs when by one thing is indicated another which is a matter of belief. The tropological or moral understanding occurs when, from something done, we learn something else that we should do. The anagogical meaning, a kind of "lifting upwards," occurs when we are shown what it is we should desire, that is, the eternal happiness of the blessed.

It is right that scripture should have this threefold sense over and above the literal sense, for this is appropriate to the subject matter of scripture, its hearer or student, its origins, and its end.

It is appropriate to its subject matter, which is doctrine, for this is concerned with God, with Christ, with the works of redemption, and with the content of belief. In terms of its substance, its subject is God; in terms of its virtue, Christ; in terms of the action described, the works of redemption; in terms of all these things together, the content of belief. Now, God is three and one: one in essence and three in person. Therefore, scripture, which is concerned with God, contains within the unity of the letter a threefold understanding. The same is true of Christ: Though the Word is one, all things are said to have been *made through him* [Jn 1:3] and shine forth in him, so that his wisdom is both manifold and one. Similarly, though the works of redemption are many, they all look toward the one principal offering of Christ. Finally, the content of belief as such sheds its light in different ways according to the differing states of believers. Scripture, then, responding to all these circumstances, gives us many-faceted meanings in the one text.

The manifold meaning of scripture is also appropriate to its hearer. For no one is a suitable hearer without being humble, pure, faithful, and attentive. So as a deterrent to pride, under the husk of the obvious literal meaning are hidden profound mystical understandings. This depth of meaning lying within the humble letter of the text abashes the arrogant, keeps out the unclean, drives away the deceitful, and arouses the idle to an understanding of the mysteries. Also, the hearers of this doctrine are not all of one kind, but are of all types—for every person who would be saved should know something of it. Scripture, therefore, has a manifold meaning so that it may win over every mind, meeting each at its own level while remaining superior to all, illuminating and setting afire with shafts of love every mind that searches it with care.

The manifold meaning of scripture is also appropriate to its source, for it came from God, through Christ and the Holy Spirit, who spoke through the prophets and the other holy people who committed this doctrine to writing. Now God speaks not only with words alone but also through deeds, because with him to say is to do and to do is to say. All created things, being the result of God's action, point toward their cause. In scripture, which has been handed on to us by God, deeds no less than words have meaning. Again, Christ the teacher, lowly though he was in the flesh, remained exalted in his divinity. It was fitting, therefore, that he and his teachings should be humble in word yet profound in meaning, just as Christ was wrapped in swaddling clothes, so the wisdom of God in scriptures should be contained in humble images. Finally, the Spirit gave enlightenment and revelations to the hearts of the prophets in various ways. No mind can remain hidden from him, and he was sent to teach the truth in its entirety. It is fitting then that his doctrine should harbor several meanings within a single passage.

It is equally appropriate to the end of scripture. For scripture was given so that we human beings might be guided in what we must know and what we must do; that we might come at last to the things for which we should hope. Because all creatures have been made to serve us in our ascent to our heavenly homeland, scripture takes on the various aspects of creatures, so that through them it might teach us the wisdom which guides us to eternal life. We are not guided to eternal life unless our intellect knows the truth we should believe, unless our will chooses the good that we should do, and unless our affections yearn to see God and to love and enjoy him. Thus, sacred scripture, given to us by the Holy Spirit, takes up the book of creation, making it relate to its own end through a threefold manner of understanding: The tropological meaning lets us know what we should resolutely do; the allegorical meaning, what we should truly believe; the anagogical meaning, what we should desire for our eternal delight. In this way, cleansed by virtuous deeds, illumined by shining faith, and made perfect by burning love, we may come at last to the prize of eternal happiness.

The Mode of Procedure of Holy Scripture

Among all the many kinds of wisdom which are contained in the breadth, length, height, and depth of sacred scripture, there is one common way of proceeding: that of authority. Grouped within this are the modes of narration, precept, prohibition, exhortation, instruction, threat, promise, supplication, and praise. All of these modes may be placed under the one general mode of proceeding by authority and quite rightly so.

This doctrine exists so that we might become good and be saved, and this is not achieved through speculation alone but by a disposition of the will. Sacred scripture, therefore, had to be handed down in the way that would dispose us best. Now, our affections are moved more strongly by examples than by arguments, by promises than by reasoning, by devotions than by definitions. This is why scripture had to avoid the mode of proceeding by definition, division, and synthesis in order to prove the properties of some subject, as do the other sciences. It had rather to adapt its own modes to the various dispositions of peoples' minds, which incline those minds differently. If some are not moved to heed precepts and prohibitions, they may be moved by the examples narrated; if they are not moved by these, they may be moved by the benefits held out to them; and if they are not moved by these, they may be moved by wise admonitions, trustworthy promises, or terrifying threats, and thus be stirred to devotion and praise of God, thereby receiving the grace which will guide them to the practice of virtuous deeds.

Now, these narrative modes cannot proceed by way of certitude based on reasoning, because particular facts do not admit of formal proof. Lest scripture seem doubtful and, consequently, lose some of its power to move, God has given it, in place of a certitude based on reasoning, a certitude based on authority, which is so great that it surpasses the keenest of human minds. The authority of one who can deceive and be deceived is not absolutely certain, and there is no one who cannot be deceived and is incapable of deceiving but God and the Holy Spirit. This is why sacred scripture, in order that it be perfectly authoritative as it should be, was handed down not through human inquiry but by divine revelation.

No passage of scripture, then, should be dismissed as useless, scorned as false, or rejected as evil, for its all-perfect author, the Holy Spirit, could not say anything false, superfluous, or trivial. This is why *heaven and earth will pass away, but* the *words* of sacred scripture *will not pass away* [Mt 24:25] without being fulfilled. *For until heaven and earth pass away, not one letter, not one stroke of a letter, will pass from the law, until it all is accomplished,* as our Savior affirms. *Therefore, whoever breaks* what scripture teaches, *and teaches others to do the same, will be called least in the kingdom of heaven; but whoever does and teaches it will be called great in the kingdom of heaven* [Mt 5:18-19].

The Mode of Expounding Holy Scripture

Scripture has this special mode of proceeding and should be understood and expounded in a way that corresponds to it. Since it hides several meanings under a single text, the expositor must *bring hidden things to light* [Jb 28:11]; that is, once a meaning has been brought forth, to clarify it through another, more evident, scriptural passage. For instance, if I were expounding the words of the psalm, *Take hold of arms and shield, and rise up to help me* [35:2], and wanted to explain what is meant by the divine "arms," I would say that these are God's truth and good will. I would then use a more explicit biblical passage to prove that this is so. For it is written elsewhere: *You have crowned us, as with a shield of your good will* [Ps 5:13], and again: *His truth shall compass you with a shield* [Ps 91:5]. No one will find this kind of thing an easy task except by long practice in reading the text and committing its literal sense to memory. Otherwise, he will never have any real capacity to expound the scriptures. The person who is too proud to learn the letters which make up a word can never understand the meaning of those words or grammatical constructions; so, too, the one who scorns the letter of sacred scripture will never rise to interpret its spiritual meanings.

The interpreter should realize, however, that one should not look for an allegorical sense everywhere, and that not everything should be given a mystical interpretation. In this regard, it must be noted that holy scripture has four parts. The first deals in a literal way with forms of being in this world, but through them signifies our redemption, as appears in the accounts of the world's creation. A second treats the actions and wanderings of the people of Israel, through which it points to the redemption of the whole human race. The third, using plain words, signifies and expresses all that concerns our redemption in terms of faith and morals. The fourth announces the mystery of this salvation, partly in plain words and partly in those which are enigmatic and obscure. Consequently, a uniform method of exposition should not be used in explaining these various parts of scripture.

In explaining holy scripture, the interpreter should be guided by three rules, which may be drawn from Augustine's *On Christian Doctrine*. The first is this: Where the primary signification of the words denote created realities or individual acts of human behavior, in the first instance they refer to the facts signified by these words, but then secondly to the mysteries of our redemption. Where the primary signification of the words expresses some aspect of faith or love, then one has no need to look for any allegorical meaning.

The second rule is this: When the words of scripture signify created realities or an aspect of the life of the people of Israel, there the interpreter must use some other part of scripture to find what each thing signifies, and then elicit the meaning of that passage using words which plainly signify some truth of our faith or of some correct principle of morality. For instance, if the text says: *The flocks of sheep all bear twins* [Sg 4:2], the interpreter must show that here "sheep" mean human beings, and "twins," the two kinds of charity.

The third rule is this: When a certain scriptural passage has a possible literal and spiritual meaning, the interpreter ought to judge whether that passage relates better to the literal or to the spiritual meaning—if, that is, it cannot be accepted in both senses. If it can be accepted in both senses, then it ought to be given both a literal and a spiritual interpretation. If it is capable of only one interpretation, then it must be taken in the spiritual sense alone. Examples of this are the statements that the law of the Sabbath has perpetual force [Ex 12:14], that the cultic priesthood is eternal [Ex 40:13], that Israel's possession of the land is unending [Gn 17:8], and that the covenant of circumcision is everlasting [Gn 17:13]. All of these statements have to be referred to their spiritual meaning.

And, bearing on this: If one is to advance through the forest of sacred scripture, hacking with an axe and thus laying it open, it is necessary that he have first acquired a knowledge of the explicitly expressed truth of the actual text of that holy scripture. In other words, one needs to know how scripture describes the beginnings, progress, and final end of the two groups of people who confront each other from opposing sides: the good, who humble themselves in this world so that they might be exalted forever in the world to come, and the wicked, who exalt themselves in this world but will be crushed eternally in the next.

Scripture, then, deals with the whole universe: high and low, first and last, and all that comes between. In a sense, it takes the form of an intelligible cross on which the whole fabric of the world can be described and in some way or another be seen in the light of the mind. To gain an understanding of this one must know about God, the origin of all things, about the creation of those things, about their fall, about their redemption through the blood of Jesus Christ, about their reformation through grace, about their healing through the sacraments, and finally about their retribution through punishment or their reward in the form of everlasting glory.

This doctrine has been handed down in such a diffuse state in the writings of the saints and the doctors that it cannot be read or heard by those who come to be taught in the subject of sacred scripture, even if they devote long periods of time to their studies. In fact, beginning theologians often dread the scripture itself, feeling it to be as confusing, orderless, and uncharted as some impenetrable forest. That is why my companions have asked me, from my own modest knowledge, to write a brief summary of the truth of theology. Yielding to their wishes, I have agreed to compose what might be called a kind of concise introduction or *breviloquium.* In it I will summarize not all topics but those items which are more important to hold, adding such explanations for understanding them as have come to mind in the course of writing.

Because theology is, indeed, discourse about God and the first Principle, as the highest science and doctrine it should resolve everything in God as its first and supreme principle. That is why, in giving the reasons for everything contained in this little work or tract, I have attempted to derive each reason from the first Principle, in order to demonstrate that the truth of sacred scripture is from God, of God, according to God, and for God as its end. It will be seen, therefore, that this science has true unity and order and that it is not improperly called theology. If, therefore, anything here is found to be imperfect, obscure, superfluous, or inaccurate, let it be imputed to pressing business, brevity of time, and poverty of knowledge; if anything is found to be good, let honor and glory be referred to God alone.

Theology, Life, and God's Word

The study of sacred scripture as the Word of God undoubtedly held pride of place in Bonaventure's education at the University of Paris. Medieval pedagogy, however, did not restrict theological inquiry to the texts of the Old and New Testaments. While the authority of the sacred scripture remained unchallenged, many theologians in the thirteenth century felt a growing urgency to complement their biblical studies with exposure to the enduring insights of authorities such as Augustine, John Damascene, Abelard, and Hugh of Saint Victor. They believed that these additional resources would enable them to examine and discuss with greater clarity the crucial questions of faith facing them, and achieve a more authentic integration of God's Word into their lives and the lives of those whom they served. Their efforts were assisted by Peter Lombard, who compiled, in the preceding century, quotations from patristic and magisterial sources and grouped them by themes in four books. The books treated the nature of God, creation and redemption, the incarnation of Christ, and the sacraments. This collection of authoritative quotes or thoughts on central theological concerns, commonly known as *The Book of Sentences,* became the standard textbook for theologians in the thirteenth century through the efforts of Bonaventure's mentor, Alexander of Hales. *The Book of Sentences* remained a classical theological resource in the classroom well into the sixteenth century.

Bonaventure was introduced to *The Book of Sentences* as early as 1243; however, it was not until he was Bachelor of Sentences in 1250 that he undertook his own commentary on Peter Lombard's four books. This new academic challenge produced the four-volume *Commentary on the Sentences,* which remains an often-neglected resource for the study of Bonaventure's spirituality. His predilection for prefaces, evident throughout his works, finds an exceptional depth and beauty of expression in the opening pages of each book of *The Commentary on the Sentences*. These prefaces are presented in this chapter. The preface to the first book serves as a general introduction to Bonaventure's interpretation of Peter Lombard's original collection of quotations. Appealing to the Aristotelian categories of material, formal, final, and efficient cause, he delineates the content, organization, intended good, and author of *The Book of Sentences*. In the second preface, Bonaventure summarizes, in magisterial fashion, the heights of human dignity at the creation of the world and the profound poverty of all who are marked by the subsequent deformity of sin. The third and fourth preface take up the question of salvation by reflecting on the power of Christ as the sacrament of redemption to restore humanity to the fullness of life, and on the individual sacraments as medicinal cures prescribed by Christ, the divine physician.

Prologue to the First Book of Sentences

The depths of rivers he has searched out and hidden things he has brought to light. [Jb 28:11]

After carefully analyzing this text from the Book of Job, the way was opened up for us to know here at the outset the four kinds of cause in the *Book of Sentences:* that is, the material, formal, final, and efficient causes. The material cause is intimated by the word rivers; the formal cause, in the phrase searching out *the depths;* the final cause, in the revelation of *hidden things;* and the efficient cause is understood from what underlies the two verbs *he has searched out* and *he has brought to light.*

The Material Cause

The material cause is signified by the word rivers. It is in the plural and not the singular, because it refers not simply to the subject matter of the books of "Sentences" as a whole, but also to the subject matter of each book taken separately. We should note that just as a real river has four characteristics, so a "spiritual river" possesses four specific qualities. In line with this fourfold distinction, there are four books of "Sentences."

When I consider that a river goes on flowing, lastingness comes into my mind. As Saint Isidore says: "A river is an unending current." When I reflect on the width of rivers, vast expanses come into my mind. In fact that is what distinguishes a river from a little brook. When I think about their movement, I find myself reflecting on circularity. As it says in the Book of Ecclesiastes: *To the place from where the rivers come, they return to flow again* [1:7]. When I consider the usefulness of rivers, I find myself thinking about processes of purification. Because of the vast amount of water they contain, rivers purify the land through which they flow without getting polluted themselves.

Every analogy is based on some similarity. Taking these four qualities metaphorically, therefore, we find that a river has a fourfold spiritual meaning, as we can gather from holy scripture.

First, then, in terms of lastingness, the emanation of the Persons in the Trinity is described as a river. This emanation uniquely is without beginning and without end. Of this river Daniel says: *The Ancient of days was seated and a swift, fiery river issued from his face* [7:9-10]. This Ancient of days is the Eternal Father, whose antiquity is his eternity. The Ancient One was seated, because he is endowed not only with eternity but also with immutability. The text says: *From the face of the Ancient One issued forth a swift, fiery river.* That is to say, from the sublime nature of his Godhead there proceeded the fullness of love and the fullness of power. The fullness of power is the Son, and thus the river was swift; the fullness of love is the Holy Spirit, and thus the river was fiery.

Secondly, in terms of vast expanses, the created world is described as a river. In fact, because of its vastness, the prophet in the Psalms calls this world not only a river, but also a sea: *So is this great sea which stretches wide its arms* [103:25]. Ezechiel says about this river: *Behold I come against you, Pharaoh, king of Egypt, great dragon who lie in the midst of your rivers and say: "The river is mine and I made myself." But I will put a bridle in your jaws* [29:6]. This great dragon, whom the Lord addresses and threatens in the figure and person of Pharaoh, king of Egypt, is the devil. He reigns over those whom he has blinded with the darkness of error, such as heretics, for instance, to whom he also says: *The river is mine and I made myself,* as if he himself made this world and had not his own origin in another. It was the devil, who framed this error and put it into the minds of the wicked Manichees, who maintain that the whole structure of the visible world was made by an evil god. The Lord will put a bridle on the jaws of this dragon when, having destroyed the power of spreading falsehood, he will manifest himself as the Creator of this river. Thus it follows in the same text of holy scripture: *And all the inhabitants of Egypt shall know that I am Lord* [29:6].

Thirdly, in terms of circularity, the incarnation of God's Son is called a river. For just as in a circle the end is joined to the beginning, so in the incarnation the highest is joined to the lowest, God to the dust of the earth, the first to the last, the eternal Son of God to human nature created on the sixth day. Of this river Sirach says: *I, like the River Dorix and like an aqueduct, came out of paradise* [24:41]. Dorix means a life-giving remedy. It is used here figuratively and may be understood conversely as the source of a life-giving remedy. For the incarnation was none other than the source of life-giving remedy for us: *Surely he has borne our infirmities and carried our sorrows* [Is 53:4]. Rightly, then, is the incarnation of the Son of God called the River Dorix. Christ says truly of himself: *I, as the River Dorix*—that is, a healing river—and *like an aqueduct, came out of paradise.* Now it is of the nature of water that as high as it rises so far does it come down. Such was the going forth of the incarnation, as the psalm says: *His going out is from the end of heaven and his circuit even to the end thereof* [18:7]. In the Gospel of John we read: *I came from the Father and have come into the world; again I am leaving the world and going to the Father* [16:28], and thus he completed a circle. A text contained in a dream which Mordecai had can be applied to this river which is Christ, taking it to refer to his coming forth from his mother: *The tiny spring that became a river and was turned into a light and into the sun* [Est 10:6]. Who, I ask you, is this tiny spring other than the most humble Virgin Mary? She became a river when she brought forth Christ who, on account of the abundance of grace he brings, is not only called a river but also the light of wisdom and the sun of justice. John says of him: *He was the true light* [1:9].

Fourthly, in terms of processes of purification, the sacramental system is called a river. The sacraments cleanse us from the stain of our sins without getting polluted themselves. Of this river, the Book of Revelation says: *He showed me the river of the water of life, bright as crystal, flowing from the throne of God and of the Lamb* [22:1]. The sacramental system is described as a river bright as crystal because of the splendor and luster the sacraments leave in the soul which has been purified in this river. It is called the river of the water of life because of the efficacy of grace which gives life to the soul. It flows from the throne of God and of the Lamb. Sacramental grace flows from God as from its author and efficient cause, and from Christ as from its mediator and meriting cause. This is why all the sacraments are said to have their efficacy from the passion of Christ. Augustine witnesses to this when he says: "From the side of Christ sleeping on the cross the sacraments came forth while the blood and water flowed out."

There is a text in the Book of Genesis which refers to all these rivers, both taken together and considered separately, which reads: *A river flowed out of Eden to water the garden and there it divided and became four rivers. . . . The name of the first is Pishon. . . . The name of the second river is Gihon. . . . And the name of the third river is Tigris. . . . And the fourth river is the Euphrates* [2:10-14]. The river flowing out of Eden is the subject matter of the whole *Book of Sentences.* The four rivers coming from it are the specific subject matter of each of the four books, as anyone can easily recognize who sets himself to explain carefully the meanings of the above-mentioned names.

Pishon means "movement of the mouth," and for this reason it refers to the emanation of the Persons. As word and breath go forth from a physical mouth, so the Son and the Holy Spirit proceed from the mouth of the Father, as it says in Sirach: *I came out of the mouth of the Most High, the firstborn before all creatures* [24:5]. These are the words of the Son himself, who is the Word and Wisdom of the Father. In the Psalms we read: *By the word the heavens were established and all the power of them by the spirit of his mouth* [32:6].

Gihon means "the sands of the seashore," and it refers as such to the created universe. As the universe of creatures is likened to the sea because of its vast expanse, so it is compared to the sands of the seashore because of the multitude of beings it contains. As it is written in Sirach: *Who has numbered the sand of the sea and the drops of rain?* [1:2].

Tigris means "an arrow," and in this it refers to the incarnation of the Son of God. Just as in an arrow iron is joined with wood, so in Christ the strength of divinity is united with the weakness of humankind. As an arrow flies through the air from a wooden bow to smite the enemy, so Christ springing from the cross destroys the adversary. This is the arrow of which the Fourth Book of Kings speaks: *The Lord's arrow of victory, the arrow of victory over Syria* [13:17].

Euphrates means "fruit bearing," and this refers to the sacramental system, which not only cleanses the soul of sin but makes it fruitful in grace. This is indicated in the Book of Revelation where it says that on both sides of the crystal river *was the tree of life . . . and the leaves of the tree were for the healing of the nations* [22:2].

The Formal Cause

As there are four rivers, so there are four deep mysteries corresponding to them. There is the deep mystery of eternal emanation which is the sublime nature of the divine being to which Ecclesiastes may be taken as referring: *It is a great depth, who shall find it out?* [7:25]. Truly God is a great depth and a deep mystery. This is what brings Paul the apostle to exclaim in Romans: *O the depth of the riches and wisdom and knowledge of God! How unsearchable are his judgments and how inscrutable his ways* [11:33]. God's judgments are indeed unsearchable because they are so deep. As the psalm says: *Your judgments are a great deep* [35:7], and we read in Sirach: *Who has measured . . . the depth of the abyss?* [1:2]. This same depth is indicated in the Book of Job: *Can you find out the deep things of God? Can you find out the limit of the Almighty? It is higher than heaven—what can you do? Deeper than Sheol—what can you know?* [11:7-8]. All of which is to say, of yourself you can do nothing, you can know nothing. Thus, Paul advises us in Ephesians: *That you, being rooted and grounded in love, may have the power to comprehend with all the saints what is the breadth and length and height and depth* [3:17-18].

The Master searches out this deep mystery in the first *Book of Sentences.* The sublime nature of the divine being consists in two things: The most awe-inspiring emanations, namely generation and procession; and the most noble qualities, which are the highest wisdom, omnipotence, and perfect love. All this forms the subject matter of the first book. In the first part he treats of the most holy Unity and Trinity of God, and in the second part, in a special treatise, he examines the three qualities just mentioned.

The deep mystery of creation is the impermanence of created being. The more a creature wastes away, whether because of sin or because of punishment, the deeper it goes into the depths. For this reason the prophet, speaking in the place of a man who has faded away because of sin, says in the psalm: *I stick fast in the mire of the deep and there is no sure standing* [68:2]. Again, the prophet prays that he may not waste away through punishment: *Let not the tempest of water drown me, nor the deep swallow me up* [68:16].

The Master searches out this deep mystery in the second book. The impermanence of created being lies in two factors: the change from non-being to being, and the reversal once more to non-being. Now, although no creature of its nature tends to non-being; nevertheless, as Augustine says, the sinner tends toward non-being because of sin. These two factors form the subject matter of the second book. In the first part he treats of the issuing forth of all things, and in the second part he deals with the fall, the temptation by the devil, original and actual sin, and so we reach the end of the book.

The deep mystery of the incarnation is the value of Christ's humanity, which was so great that it can truly be described as deep, as having no limit, as inexhaustible. A text from Jonah may be applied to this deep mystery: *You did cast me into the deep, into the heart of the sea, and a flood encompassed me* [2:4]. This can be understood of Christ, for he was so humbled that he can truly be said to have been cast into the deep and degraded. We read in Isaiah: *We have seen him, and there is no sightliness that we should be desirous of him. Despised and the most abject of men, a man of sorrows, and acquainted with infirmity* [53:2-3]. He describes himself accurately, therefore, as cast forth. But where is he cast? Into the depths of the sea and the depths of a river. The passion of Christ may be likened to the sea because of the bitterness of his sufferings, and likened to a river because of the sweetness of his love. For the heart of Jesus was so affected toward us by the tenderness of love, that it did not seem too much to him to undergo the worst and most bitter death for our sake.

The Master searches out this deep mystery in the third book. The value of Christ consists in two things: namely, his sufferings, by which he redeemed us; and his actions, by which he formed us and which consist in the works of the virtues, the gifts, and the commandments. These form the subject matter of the third book. The first part treats of the incarnation and passion in which is found our salvation; and the second part treats of the virtues, the gifts, and the commandments, in which is contained our formation.

The deep mystery of the sacramental system is the power of perfect healing. So great in fact is the efficacy of sacramental healing that it is beyond the human mind to comprehend it, and so it may rightly be described as a deep mystery. Of this Isaiah says: *You made the depths of the sea a way for the redeemed to pass over* [51:10]. This depth in which the Egyptians were submerged and which the children of Israel, delivered from Egypt, passed over, is the efficacy of the sacraments, in which the works of darkness are destroyed and the armor of light and the gifts of grace conferred, through which we pass from the power of darkness into the kingdom of the children of God's love. The efficacy of the sacraments is compared to the depth of the sea and the depth of a river. Of the sea, because it first delivers us from sin and leads us to the bitterness of penance; of a river, because it delivers us from wretchedness and leads us to the delights of glory. This was graphically prefigured in the children of Israel, for whom, as they left Egypt, the sea dried up and they went across *on dry ground in the midst of the sea,* as Exodus tells us [15:19]. When they entered the Promised Land, the river dried up and they passed over the Jordan, as is written in Joshua [4:22-23].

The Master searches out this deep mystery in the fourth book. The power of perfect healing has two components: the curing of the diverse weaknesses that assail us, and liberation from all the miseries that plague us. These two components form the subject matter of the whole of the fourth book. The first part treats of the various kinds of healing which the seven sacraments bring about. The second part deals with that perfect healing: the glory of the risen life to which they come who truly and faithfully received the sacraments of the Church; and, on the other hand, it deals with the punishments of the wicked who despised the sacraments of the Church.

The Final Cause

After searching out the four deep mysteries in the four books, there emerges the purpose or final cause, that is, the revelation of four hidden mysteries.

The first is the mystery of the divine nature of which Isaiah says: *Truly, you are a hidden God, the God of Israel, the Savior* [45:15]. The majesty of the divine nature is indeed hidden for us, as it is written in the Book of Job: *How small a whisper do we hear of him! But the thunder of his power who can understand?* [26:14]. For certain no one can understand this, except him with whom the wisdom of God dwells. This is the reason why that lover of wisdom, the author of the Book of Wisdom, made this prayer: *Send her forth from your holy heavens and from the throne of your glory send her* [9:10].

The Master, filled with wisdom from on high, brings this hidden mystery to light in the course of his investigations in the first book. He examines and unfolds the most awe-inspiring emanations and the most noble qualities of the

Godhead, and so he reveals to us, as far as it is possible while we are in this world, the majesty of the divine nature.

The second hidden mystery is the order of divine wisdom, of which Job speaks: *But where is wisdom to be found? And where is the place of understanding? It is hid from the eyes of all living* [28:12, 20-21]. Indeed wisdom is hidden, for as Job also says: *But wisdom is drawn out of secret places* [28:18]. To know wisdom it is necessary to search out its depths, not in itself, but in its works in which it shines forth. So it says in the Book of Sirach: *There is one most high Creator, and he poured her out upon all his works* [1:8-10].

The Master reveals this hidden mystery in his analyses in the second book. He examines the order of good and evil and makes known to us how the wisdom of God *was set up from all eternity and of old before the earth was made* [Prv 8:23].

The third hidden mystery is the strength of divine power of which Habakuk says: *Horns are in his hands: there is his strength hid* [3:4]. He is speaking there about Christ hanging on the cross where the strength of his power was hidden under the veil of weakness. This *is the plan of the mystery hidden for ages* of which Ephesians speaks: *To me, grace was given to preach to the Gentiles the unsearchable riches of Christ and to make all men see what is the plan of the mystery hidden for ages in God* [3:8-9]. This is the hidden mystery, the sacred secret, that the mighty God was clothed with the protection of our weakness in order to overcome the enemy. This is unheard of since the world began.

The investigations of the third book made known the strength of the divine power. It shows how Christ in his weakness overcomes the opposing power. If he was victorious by weakness, what would have happened if he had entered the fight with his power? If *the weakness of God is stronger than men* [1 Cor 1:25], *who shall turn back* [Is 14:27] the arm of God? It is abundantly clear that his power is indescribable whose weakness is so strong.

The fourth hidden mystery is the sweetness of the divine mercy of which the psalmist says: *How great is the abundance of your sweetness, O Lord, which you have hidden for those who fear you*

[30:20]. Indeed, the sweetness of mercy is hidden and stored up for those who fear God because, as the psalmist says: *The mercy of the Lord is from everlasting to everlasting upon those who fear him* [102:17] *and on those who hope in his mercy* [146:11].

This sweetness is revealed in the analyses contained in the fourth book. He unfolds how God forgives our sins in the present, what cures he applies to our wounds, and what gifts he will grant us in the future. In this way the Master makes known to us the sweetness of divine mercy.

The Efficient Cause

The unveiling of these hidden mysteries is the aim of the four books as a whole. With this intention in mind for himself and for his readers, the Master of Sentences *searched out the depths of rivers* under the guidance of the Holy Spirit. The Holy Spirit himself is the chief searcher of secret things and of the depths, as Paul tells us: *For the Spirit searches all things, even the depths of God* [1 Cor 2:10]. Inflamed with the love of this Spirit and enlightened by his radiance and splendor, the Master composed this work and *searched out the depths of rivers.* By the aid of this same Spirit he became a revealer of hidden mysteries. It is he of whom Daniel says: *He reveals deep and hidden things and knows what is in darkness* [2:22].

This was the Master's aim and intention, as he himself explains in the Prologue: "Wishing to place the light of truth on the candle stand, we composed this volume with God's help and much work and effort from the witnesses to truth who are established in eternity." A short while before that, he had outlined his purpose as follows: "To unfold the hidden truths of theological investigations."

So, from the foregoing reflections, it is evident what are the material, formal, final, and efficient causes of the *Book of Sentences*.

Prologue to the Second Book of Sentences

Only this have I found: that God made the human person upright, and he has entangled himself in an infinity of questions [Eccl 7:30].

The words just quoted from the wise man in Ecclesiastes provide a response to those anxious to consider the principal intention and entire contents of the second *Book of Sentences.* When someone has attempted to follow wisdom in all matters, and failed more often than succeeded, it is necessary to acknowledge what has been discovered: *that God made the human person upright, and he has entangled himself in an infinity of questions.* This statement encompasses two realities: upright formation and rectitude come from God, since *God made the human person upright,* and the miserable deformation of humankind originates in the human person, since *he has entangled himself in an infinity of questions.* These two statements encompass the goal of all human understanding: to recognize the origin of good, to seek it out, reach it, and rest in it; and to know the source and origin of evil, so as to avoid it and guard against it. These matters include the whole intention of this book, namely two things: the original condition of humankind and the subsequent fall from that state.

The Original State of Humankind

God made the human person upright tells us of the original human state. The *manner* in which God made humankind upright is explained by Sirach: *God created the human person from the earth* refers to the body; *and made him after his own image* refers to nature of the soul; *and he turned him into it again* refers to the addition of grace [17:1-2]. This grace turns the soul toward God by means of habits, called virtues; therefore, it states *and clothed him with strength according to himself.* These words demonstrate that God not only made rectitude possible for men and women by conferring his image upon them, but actually made them upright by turning them toward him. A person is upright when understanding is in accord with the highest truth in the act of knowing, the will is conformed to the highest good in the act of loving, and strength is joined with the highest power in operating. This occurs when someone turns completely away from self and toward God.

A person is upright, first of all, when understanding is in accord with the highest truth. When I say "in accord," however, I do not mean completely, rather a type of imitation. If, as Anselm says, "truth is rectitude perceivable to the mind alone," and nothing equals uprightness like that which is upright, then when our intellect is in accord with the truth, it is necessarily rectified. The intellect is brought into accord when it actually turns toward the truth. Actual truth is defined as "the accord between perception and reality." When our understanding is turned toward truth it is made true and thus in accord with truth, just as it is made upright when it is in accord with rectitude. Augustine's book, *The True Religion,* states: "Without truth, no one judges rightly." But the one who looks to the truth judges rightly, as the Lord said to Simon: *You have judged rightly* [Lk 7:43]; that is, "you have decided properly."

Likewise, a person is "rectified" as the will is conformed to the highest good. The highest good is the highest equity or justice; for one becomes better as one becomes more just. Anselm, however, says: "Justice is the rectitude of the will." Nothing, however, conforms to uprightness as that which is upright; therefore, as long as the will is shaped in harmony with the highest good and equity, it is certainly rectified. The will is conformed when it turns, in love, toward the good. As Hugh of Saint Victor says: "I know, soul of mine, that when you love something, you are transformed into its likeness." The one who loves goodness is upright. This is what the Song of Songs states: *The upright love you* [1:3]; that is to say, "the upright turn toward your goodness while your goodness inclines toward them." The soul that has experienced this cries out and says:

How good God is to Israel, to those who are of an upright heart! [Ps 72:1]. And since it is only the upright who are experienced in this regard, it is said: *Praise is fitting for the upright* [Ps 32:1].

A person is no less rectified when his or her power is joined with the highest power. "Something is *upright* whose mean does not extend beyond extremes." The extremes are the *first and last, alpha and omega, beginning and end* [Rv 22:13]. The action by which an agent reaches the goal is found in the middle. That power is therefore "upright" whose operation is from the first principle to the last end. Since divine power is operative in all things and works on God's account, it is the most upright of all operations. Nothing joins with what is upright except the upright; and so, when power joins with the highest power it undoubtedly becomes upright. As a result, a human being is not only made upright but is also made *ruler* and *king* as suggested in Deuteronomy: *He will be king with the most upright: the princes of the people being assembled with the tribes of Israel* [33:5]. This will happen in glory, when our power will be joined to the divine power. We will have complete power then over our wills, just as God has over his. Consequently all are kings and promised the kingdom of heaven.

God, therefore, made men and women upright when he turned them toward himself. In their turning toward God, they became upright not only in relation to things above them but also in relation to things beneath them. Men and women stand in the middle. While they are turned in the direction of God and subject to him, everything else is subject to them. This is so because God subjected every created truth to their intellect for discernment, every good to their affections for use, every force to their power for governance.

Indeed it follows that human understanding, once it encounters divine truth, lays claim to the wisdom by which all things are discerned. For according to the Book of Wisdom: *He gave me the knowledge of all things that I might know: the disposition of the whole world, and the power of the elements; the beginning, and ending, and in-between of the times, the alterations of their courses, and the changes of the seasons; the cycle of the year, and the order of the* stars; *the nature of living creatures, and the rage of wild animals, the force of the winds, and reasoning of humankind, the diversity of plants, and the power of roots; such things hidden and unforeseen* [7:17-21]. And so Adam gave names to all things.

God subjected, nonetheless, all things to human will for their use so that they might utilize everything to their advantage. As the psalm says: *He has put all things under his feet* [8:8]. Likewise in the First Letter to the Corinthians, the apostle, when speaking to those already turned toward God, states: *Everything is for you* [3:22]. According to Genesis, God also subjected everything to the power of humankind for governance: *Subdue it, and rule over the fishes of the sea and the birds of the air* [1:28].

The upright condition of the human person in relation to things above and below is touched upon in the passage: *Let us make the human person to our image and likeness; and let him have dominion,* etc. [Gn 1:26]. God made men and women upright, therefore, when he turned toward them and made them similar to himself, thus placing them over everything. This clearly reveals that upright condition of humankind.

The Poverty of Humankind

What follows brings to mind the miserable deviation of the human person: *he has entangled himself in an infinity of questions.* Here we note the *way* humankind fell as well as the *state* into which it fell. The manner of the fall is indicated by three aspects of sin and three points in the text. Sin entails *a turning from, a turning toward,* and *a loss of goods* or *stripping.* In the text "entangling" refers to *the turning toward,* "infinity" to *the turning from,* and "questions" to *a stripping.* The act of *turning toward* renders men and women impure, the *turning from* leaves them weak, and a *stripping* reduces them to poverty. All this is contained in the words: *he has entangled himself in an infinity of questions.*

We also note the state into which humanity fell. Although men and women fell from uprightness to the extent of losing uprightness itself, they did not lose the aptitude for it. They lost the habit of uprightness without losing the inclination to it. The similitude was lost, nevertheless, *he passes like an image* [Ps 38:7]. Men and women became anxious searchers, because the inclination remained without the habit. No created object could compensate for the good lost, since it was infinite, and so the human person desires, seeks, but never rests. Thus by turning away from uprightness *he entangled himself in an infinity of questions*.

The understanding, by turning away from the highest truth, becomes ignorant; it enmeshes itself in endless questions through curiosity. As Ecclesiastes says: *There are those who day and night take no sleep with their eyes. I understand that man can find no reason of all those words of God* [8:16-17], which, one might add, could put an end to his desires and inquiries. Indeed, one question leads to another, provokes a new debate, and those asking the question are entangled in inextricable doubts. That is why Proverbs states: *It is an honor for a man to separate himself from quarrels; but all fools are meddling with reproaches* [20:3]. Miserable are they who, according to the First Letter to Timothy, pay attention *to fables and endless genealogies that prompt questions* [1:4]. The Second Letter to Timothy notes that these people, by their very nature, provoke abuse, because they are *ever learning and never attaining to the knowledge of the truth* [3:7].

The will, by opposing the highest good, becomes destitute as concupiscence and greed entangle it in an infinite number of questions. As Proverbs says: *The fire never says, It is enough* [30:16] and Ecclesiastes adds: *A covetous man will not be satisfied with money* [5:9]. So the human person is endlessly asking and begging. Covetousness, likewise, is never satisfied. Instead, it is entwined in endless questions dealing with the desire for pleasure. Wisdom states: *All things are mixed together, blood, murder, theft and guile, corruption and unfaithfulness, tumults and perjury, disturbing the good, forgetfulness of God, defiling of souls, changing of nature, disorder in marriage, and the irregularity of adul-*

tery and uncleanness [14:25-26]. These are the countless questions, all mingled together, in which humankind involves itself, once the will is no longer conformed to the highest good. Human power, by breaking away from the highest power, becomes weak. Entangled in endless questions through its instability, it constantly seeks rest but never finds it. *The Lord mingled in the midst of Egypt the spirit of dizziness* [19:14] according to Isaiah. This is the spirit of instability, and everything is off balance because of it. So the sinful person is *like dust, which the wind drives from the face of the earth* [Ps 1:4]. This is why the psalm says: *If you turn away your face, they shall be troubled; you shall take away their breath* [103:29]. The sinful person is likewise similar to the dust which the wind drives from the face of the earth. Just as dust cannot settle in a whirlwind, neither can our power remain steady. This is why it seeks out and moves on from innumerable places as it begs for support.

Humankind, then, entangled itself in an infinity of questions through curiosity, falling from truth into ignorance; through covetousness, falling from goodness into evil; through instability, falling from power into impotence. The original state of humankind and subsequent fall are intimated, in this manner, by the text cited at the beginning. I have found this to be the sole matter treated in this second *Book of Sentences.*

Prologue to the Third Book of Sentences

> *But God, who is rich in mercy, by reason of his very great love, with which he has loved us, even when we were dead by reason of our sins, brought us to life together with Christ, by whose grace you have been saved.* [Eph 2:4-5]

This passage is written in the Letter to the Ephesians [2:4-5]. Here the mystery of our redemption is made known to us. Here too the subject matter of the *Book of Sentences* is clearly shown to us, especially that of its third part in which the sacrament of our redemption achieved through Christ is explained. There are four points pertinent to the restoration of the human race that can be noted in this passage: the first of which is the author of the restoration; the second, the restorable fall; the third, the person of the Restorer; the fourth and last, the salvation of the restored person.

The Restoration of Humankind

The author of the restoration is indicated when it is said: *But God, who is rich in mercy* . . . etc. In his overflowing mercy, and not by some other moving force, he arranged to restore the human race as it is written in the third chapter of John: *God so loved the world that he gave his only-begotten Son, that those who believe in him may not perish* [3:16].

The restorable fall is indicated because it is said: *Even when we were dead by reason of our sins*. For the sin of our first parents was the cause of our death, through which the entire human race fell from the state of innocence, according to what has been written to the Romans: *As through one man sin entered into the world and through sin, death, and thus death has passed to all men because all have sinned* [5:12]. Because they sinned in another and through another, that fall was, therefore, restorable.

The person of the Restorer is indicated through the following passage: *He has brought us to life together with Christ*. It was Christ in whom that restoration has been achieved, as has been written in Colossians: *It has pleased God the Father that in him all his fullness should dwell, and that through him he should reconcile to himself all things, whether on the earth or in the heavens, making peace through the blood of his cross* [1:19-20].

The salvation of the restored person is touched on by what is said: *By whose grace you have been saved*. For efficacy was given to the sacraments through the merit of the passion of Christ, so that healing grace is given to the sick through it, according to Titus: *But according to his mercy, he saved us through the bath of regeneration and renewal by the Holy Spirit; whom he has abundantly poured out upon us through Jesus Christ our Savior* [3:5-6].

These four points are considered together in Romans in a passage where it says: *But God commends his charity toward us*—behold the author of the restoration—*because when as yet we were sinners*—behold the restorable fall—*Christ died for us*—in which the person of the Restorer is indicated—*Much more now that we are justified by his blood, shall we be saved through him from the wrath*—behold the salvation of the restored person [5:8-9].

According to these four points, provided by the aforementioned passage, there are four books of "Sentences." In the first book, the author of the restoration is treated, that is, the blessed Trinity. In the second, the restorable one, that is, the person falling from the state of integrity and innocence. In the third, the person of the Restorer is considered, that is Christ, God and man. In the fourth, the salvation of the restored person, which certainly consists in the expiation of the fault and the removal of all misery.

Christ as the Mediator of Life

Thus, it is evident how this entire book treats the explanation of the mystery of our restoration. Nevertheless, in a more special manner, it looks to the third book in which it is shown how we have been brought to life through Christ. The apostle makes this known in that aforementioned passage when he says: *He has brought us to life together with Christ.* The apostle says this because God brings us to life *in* Christ, *with* Christ, *through* Christ, and *according* to Christ.

In the first place, God has brought us to life *in* Christ, because he has shared our mortality of life in his person, according to that passage in John: *As the Father has life in himself, even so he has given to the Son to have life in himself* [5:26]. Therefore, if the Son has life in himself, while he has taken to himself our mortality, he has joined us to the true and immortal life, and through this he has brought us to life *in* himself.

He has brought us to life *with* Christ, while Christ himself, who was life, lived among mortal men, according to that passage in the beginning of the First Epistle of John: *What was from the beginning, what we have seen with our eyes, what we have looked upon and our hands have handled: We speak of the Word of Life; and the Life was made known and we have seen, and now testify and announce to you life eternal* [1:1-2]. So *while he was seen on earth and lived among men* [Bar 3:38], God brought us to life *with* Christ, when he made us live with him.

He also brought us to life *through* Christ, when he snatched us from death through his death, according to that passage of the First Epistle of Peter: *Christ also died once for sins, the just for the unjust, that he might bring us to God. Put to death indeed in the flesh, he was brought to life in the spirit* [3:18]. When Christ laid down his life for us, God brought the dead human race to life through him.

Finally, he brought us to life *according* to Christ when he guided us through the path of life according to his example, according to that passage of the psalmist: *You have made known to me the paths of life* [15:10]. He made known to us the paths of life when he gave us faith, hope, charity, and the gifts of grace. To these he added the commands according to which Christ himself walked and in which the path of life consists. It is according to these that Christ has taught us to walk. God has brought us to life *according* to Christ because he guides his imitators to life.

The four of these points are found together in the second chapter of the Letter to the Philippians: *He emptied himself, taking the form of a slave*—behold the first, namely, that he united our mortality to his life—*was made in the likeness of men*—behold the second, namely, that he lived with humankind as a man—*he humbled himself even to death*—behold the third, namely, that he freed us from death through his death—*because of this God exalted him*—behold the fourth, namely, that after death he had many followers and imitators who believed in him [2:7].

Prologue to the Fourth Book of Sentences

The druggist will make sweet confections and will make up ointments of health. [Sir 38:7]

Those words are written in Sirach and, if thought of carefully, explain and set off the subject matter of the fourth *Book of Sentences* in furtherance of our education and training. The explanation comes through a twofold metaphor or figure of speech: namely, *sweet confections* and *ointments of health*. By these we are given to understand that the medicine, which the sacraments are, is pleasant as well as wholesome. Here we have a first-rate estimation of both the physician and his remedy. All a patient looks for in a medicine is that it be pleasant to take and effective as a cure. The ideal physician's medicine has both of these traits; as the poet said: "That man took every score there was who mixed the useful with the sweet." The sacraments as medicine, therefore, are sweet confections and ointments of health. As ointments of health, they relate to the cure of the patient; as sweet confections, they are concerned with pleasing God. As such they are opposed to the two aspects of wrongdoing: namely, offending God and damaging nature. It is by offending God that the human person is stripped of grace, and by damaging nature that wounds are inflicted on his humanity. The sacraments are, therefore, ideal remedies. They have the sweet quality that finds acceptance with God, thereby making reparation and petitioning for grace. They also clothe persons in their nakedness, possess the power to look after them in their sickness, and thus restore their humanity.

The Fragrance of the Sacraments

It is like the man going down from Jerusalem to Jericho and being stripped and left wounded but dressed again and healed by the Samaritan. That Samaritan is Christ the Lord. In his person is this statement made: *The druggist shall make sweet confections*, that is to say, he will institute fragrant sacraments which would be agreeable to the divine majesty. *He shall make*, it says, in the future tense since this was spoken at the time of the Mosiac Law in reference to the age of the law of grace. Even if you say confections and sacrifices fragrant to God were offered in times past, still it was not due to their inherent worth that they were acceptable to God. The Lord commanded Moses, in the Book of Exodus, to make incense compounded by the work of the perfumer: *You shall make incense*, etc. [30:35]. He commanded Aaron to offer incense: *You shall set the altar over against the veil* [30:6]; *and after that, he said: And Aaron shall burn incense upon it in the morning . . . in the evening he shall burn an everlasting incense* [30:7, 8]. In Leviticus, the phrase for *a most sweet savor to the Lord* recurs in regard to almost all oblations [cf. Lv 1:13; 2:2; 6:21; 23:18]. This was a perfume, however, which did not find acceptance with the Lord because of the insufficiencies in the sacrifices of the Law, that had, as the apostle points out, merely *a shadow of the good things to come* [Heb 10:1]. They were not pleasing, because of the uncleanness of the offerers as Isaiah says: *Offer sacrifice no more in vain: incense is an abomination to me* [1:13]. The reason he gives is: *Your hands are full of blood* [1:15].

If anybody is going to make sweet-smelling confections, he had better be free from all uncleanness and be filled with a scent that has true fragrance in it. Such was not to be had by, nor could it be produced by, men and women, because they would be unclean producers. So the Lord by his own power had to fit them with bodies, as we read in psalm 39, which the apostle applies to Christ: *As he comes into the world, he says, No sacrifice, no offering was your demand; you have fitted me, instead, with a body. You have not found any pleasure in burnt sacrifices, in sacrifice for sin. See then, I said, I am coming* [Heb 10:5-7]. *Fitted* is well said, for that all-clean Lord, as he made the Virgin clean "with a purity greater than which, under God, is unthinkable," fitted him with a body. He was to be a vessel of cleanliness containing every fragrance. The patriarch Jacob, in Genesis, with a presentiment of this, pronounced: *The smell of my son is as the smell of a plentiful field which the Lord has blessed* [27:27]. No, Christ was the perfect dealer in unguents; he did not go begging his scent elsewhere, but was himself redolent of the Father. Filled as he was with that scent, to pass it on to others he offered himself for us all to God the Father, according to Ephesians: *He loved us and gave himself on our behalf, a sacrifice breathing out fragrance as he offered it to God* [5:2]. It was then that the alabaster box was broken and the whole house was scented with the ointment. It was then that we all received something out of this abundance since God propitiated, not only by the passion itself, but even by what constitutes "memorials" of the passion. It is not alone the passion that is a "sweet confection," but so are also those things that call it to mind: namely, the sacraments. This is in line with what we read in Sirach: *The memory of Josias is like the composition of a sweet smell made by the art of a perfumer* [49:1]. Josias here standing for the suffering Christ, for the name Josias means "where the Lord's incense is" or "to whom belongs the Lord's sacrifice". The sacraments are memorial signs of the passion that was accomplished in the past. The house of the Church militant is filled to overflowing with these memorials. So it is filled with the odor of the ointment in accordance with what the Holy Spirit says in the Song of Songs: *The sweet smell of your ointments is above all aromatic spices* [4:40]. The druggist, therefore, *shall make sweet confections*, ones, that is, that are pleasing to God.

The Curative Power of the Sacraments

In no less a fashion shall he make up ointments of health: namely, sacraments which cure disease. In the Law, you did certainly have anointings which were symbolic, though they were not curative; the anointing was superficial, while the disease was lethal. On this point, the apostle tells the Hebrews that the legal remedies have no power *where conscience is con-*

cerned, to bring the worshiper to his full growth; they are but outward observances, connected with food and drink and ceremonial washings on this occasion or that [Heb 9:9]. It was because their anointings were on the flesh, whereas the lethal wound was in the soul, that they were powerless as remedies. *That sins should be taken away by the blood of bulls and goats is impossible* [Heb 10:4]. You have Isaiah, too, crying out in his first chapter: *Wounds and bruises and swelling sores are not bound up, nor dressed nor fomented with oil* [1:6]. He is referring to the three kinds of sin constituting man's illness: *wounds* are original sin, *bruises* are venial sin, and *swelling sores* are mortal sin. This is why just before that, he said: *The whole head is sick, and the whole heart is sad* [1:5].

With regard to this, then, if anybody is going to make health-giving ointments, he had better produce an anointing that is spiritual and one that has vital efficacy in it. Christ the Lord was the one to do it; he was the true "Christus," the anointed one, as in Isaiah: *The Spirit of the Lord is upon me, for he has anointed me. He has sent me to preach to the meek*, etc. [61:1]. That this is to be interpreted as referring to Christ he himself is the witness in the fourth chapter of Luke, where, after reading out that text, he said: *This scripture which I have read in your hearing is today fulfilled* [4:21]. He is the one who had power to make up a healing ointment, according to what Saint Peter says of him in Acts: *God anointed him with the Holy Spirit and with power, so that he went about doing good, and curing all those who were under the devil's tyranny, for God was in him* [10:38]. He anointed him *with the Holy Spirit*, so he produced that spiritual ointment; he anointed him *with power*, hence its vital efficacy. Through his anointing, God was in him; he himself being God and thus having life in himself: *As the Father has within him the gift of life, so he has granted to the Son that he too should have within him the gift of life* [Jn 5:26].

Because he had life within himself, he had power to revive those who were dead. So he made ointments which were cures for lethal disease. It was when he united our mortal nature with life, that he, who was life, died. Then was that confection made, in which and by means of which he who was dead finds life again. It is from his death that the sacraments derive their life-giving efficacy. In connection with the text in Ephesians, *This is a great sacrament, and I am applying it here to Christ and his Church* [5:32], Augustine's words are these: "Adam sleeps that Eve may appear; Christ dies, that the Church may appear. Eve was made out of the side of the sleeping Adam; the Church was formed by the mysteries that flowed from the lance-pierced side of the dead Christ." It is more fitting to speak of the sacraments as emanating from the "side" than from the feet or hands—blood flowed from these—because a more suitable sign is implied, in that blood and water came forth together. Moreover, they flowed out of one who was already dead. This offers a rather fitting description of the constitution and institution of the sacraments. The vital blood flowed forth with water: This means the sacraments acquire their efficacy when death is joined to life. The sacraments are instituted with "word" and "element" together; so we speak of them as being not only "made" but "made up" for healing.

These sacraments, therefore, are perfect cures. Our druggist made these *sweet* confections to be agreeable to God. He made them, these *ointments of* health, to cure the sickness of humankind. They are healing anointings, because they both confer health and make us ready for health. They confer the basic health we need, the health that comes with grace, of which the psalm speaks: *He heals the broken-hearted, and binds up all their wounds* [146:3]. They make us ready to receive perfect health, the health that comes with glory, of which another psalm speaks: *It is he who forgives all your guilt, who heals every one of your ills* [102:3]. He does this in the life of glory.

The Cultivation of God's Word

As an expression of evangelical spirituality, the Franciscan way of life embraced by Bonaventure considered preaching to be an essential dimension of ministry. The origin of the Franciscan community around the year 1209, according to the early biographers of Francis of Assisi, was linked inseparably with the gospel mandate to announce the kingdom of God throughout the world. Francis and his friars earned a deserved reputation for a simple, direct style of preaching that moved people everywhere to dedicate themselves to following Christ, the Word of God. The formal Rule of Life for the Franciscan community, composed in 1221 and revised in 1223, followed the prescriptions of the Fourth Lateran Council of 1215 and urged friars to proclaim the word of God in conformity with the guidelines of the Roman Catholic Church. This ministerial injunction necessitated a formal theological education and opened the door to numerous, learned Franciscans, beginning with the noted theologian and evangelist, Anthony of Padua, to undertake the instruction of the friars. Bonaventure's *Commentary on the Gospel of Luke* underscores his commitment to the formation of educated preachers, while his numerous sermons testify to his passion for preaching.

The three sermons of Bonaventure presented in this chapter employ metaphors linked with the planting, cultivation, and harvest of God's word. These agrarian images are grounded in Bonaventure's conception of preaching as sowing the divine seed. The first sermon speaks of the seed of God's word scattered throughout the fields of human conscience. This seed bears the fruit of grace when heard with reverence and put into practice. The second sermon compares the word of God to sunlight. Just as the rays of the sun encourage a tree to bring forth a harvest of good fruit, divine speech enlightens the soul and fosters an abundance of good works. God's word illuminates the soul through the understanding of truth, inflames the soul with love, and strengthens the soul with hope. Receptivity is a major theme of the third sermon. The seed of God's word is unable to germinate in the human heart if the tangled weeds of sin remain. Contrition begins the necessary task of rooting out sin and is followed by mortification and the desire for God. Only then may God's word be heard with reverence, embraced with fidelity, and practiced in good deeds. The harvest is evident, Bonaventure says, in the purity, understanding and intimacy with Christ, the Word of God, enjoyed by those whose hearts have provided good soil for the seed of God's word.

Sermon for the Fifth Sunday
after the Epiphany

The kingdom of heaven may be compared to a man who sowed good seed in his field. [Mt 13:24]

Then Elijah arose, a prophet burning like fire, and his word blazed like a torch [Sir 48:1]. This passage from the Book of Sirach aptly describes the prophet Elijah, who would harshly reprove erring sinners, but at the same time would set before them the word of truth. It also lets us understand several things about the task of preaching. First, it tells us that the preacher must rise above all carnal-mindedness, so that he might delight the angelic hosts; this is indicated by the words: *then Elijah arose.* He must also be inflamed with charity, so that he might burn within for the salvation of all people, as we see when it says: *burning like fire.* Finally, he must be resplendent through a holy manner of life, so that he might outwardly shed light on the minds of his neighbors, as we see in the following phrase: *and his word blazed like a torch.*

My dear friends, I am neither free from carnal desires, nor am I wholly inflamed with the fire of love, and my life is certainly far from being resplendent in holiness. Therefore, before I say anything else, let us implore our tender and compassionate God, so that according to his mercy he might sever me from worldly desires, enkindle me with love, and bestow on me the light of his holiness. Thus, forgetting my earthly passions, inflamed with divine love and shining with the splendor of holiness, I might speak with you a while for the glory of God and the salvation of our souls.

The kingdom of heaven may be compared to a man who sowed good seed in his field. According to the blessed Dionysius, "the divine ray can enlighten us only by being concealed in a variety of sacred veils." So our Lord Jesus Christ, knowing that it would be more beneficial for our sight-impaired race, chose in today's text to explain the marvelous work of the creation of humankind through the apt metaphor of a man sowing good seed in his field. Indeed the Lord *sowed good seed in his field* when, in the field which is the fabric of the world, he made humankind *according to his own image and likeness* [Gn 1:26]. This excellent metaphor captures several dimensions of this creation: its operative principle, through the image of the man; its receptive subject, through the symbol of the field; and the intermediate act, through the sowing of good seed. First of all, the operative principle of creation is expressed when our Lord says: *The kingdom of heaven may be compared to a man.* That "man," metaphorically speaking, is God. Second, the receptive subject of the creation of humankind is indicated when the passage continues with *in his field.* The field is the fabric of this world. Finally, the intermediate creative act is inferred in the words: *sowed good seed,* inasmuch as God created humankind according to his own image and likeness.

The Operative Principle of Creation: the Origin, Means, and End

Let us turn to the first point. It says: *The kingdom of heaven may be compared to a man:* This metaphor of "a man" indicates the operative principle of creation. Now, anything is understood truly and perfectly when one knows its origin, its means, and its end. And so, if we wish to comprehend perfectly the creation of humankind, at least insofar as the limitations of our minds permit, we must come to an understanding of our origin, our means, and our end. As we have seen, it is only then that one can arrive at a truly complete knowledge of a thing. Now the source of creation—not simply of humankind but of the whole universe—is the operation of a power making all things supernaturally; its means is the guidance of a wisdom ordering all things harmoniously; and its end is the consummation of a mercy and a justice rendering to all things according to their merits. Therefore, we will first examine the creation of humankind as the act of a power which serves as its operative principle by means of the story of the man sowing good seed in his field; second we will examine the governance of wisdom as its directive intends through the story of the head of the household who brings laborers into his vineyard; and third, the consummation of mercy and justice, as creation's final end, through the story of the king settling accounts with his servants.

First of all, let us look at the creation of humankind insofar as it is the product of a power serving as its operative principle by means of the story of the man sowing good seed in his field. Thus Matthew tells us: *The kingdom of heaven may be compared to someone who sowed good seed in his field, but while people were asleep, an enemy came and sowed weeds among the wheat* [13:24-25]. The Lord *sowed good seed in his field*; namely, in the fabric of the world, when he created humankind in his own image and likeness; but *an enemy*, namely the devil, *while people were asleep*—now this refers to Adam and Eve, who were neglectful in observing the commands of God—*sowed weeds*, that is, vices and sins, from which were born *children of wrath* [Eph 2:3]. This exposition is based on the words of the Lord himself, for the passage continues: *And his disciples approached him, saying, "Explain to us the parable of the weeds of the field." He answered, "The one who sows the good seed is the Son of Man, the field is the world, and the good seed are the children of the kingdom; the weeds are the children of the evil one, and the enemy who sowed them is the devil"* [Mt 13:36-39].

The second aspect, the governance of wisdom serving as creation's directive means, may be illustrated through the story of the head of the household who brings laborers into his vineyard. In Matthew we read: *For the kingdom of heaven is like a landowner who went out early in the morning to hire laborers for his vineyard,* and so on [20:1-16]. This parable describes the reign of God from its beginning until its end, for it tells us that he invited workers into his vineyard at five different times; namely *early in the morning . . . at the third hour . . . the sixth hour . . . the ninth hour . . . and at the eleventh hour.* He sent workers *early in the morning* when he gave the natural law; *at the third hour* when he gave the written Law; *at the sixth hour*, when he sent prophets to teach the people; *at the ninth hour* when he gave the New Law, sending his apostles to *preach* it *to every creature* [Mk 16:15]; and *at the eleventh hour* when, following the apostles, he sent preachers and teachers, and indeed keeps sending them, until the very end.

The third aspect, the consummation of mercy and justice, which represents creation's final end, may be seen in the story of the ruler who wished to tally his servants' accounts. Again, Matthew tells us: *The kingdom of heaven may be compared to a king who wished to settle accounts with his servants,* and so on [18:23-35]. Now in this parable, the operation of divine mercy is illustrated in the forgiveness of the debt, the work of divine justice in the condemnation of the *wicked servant*. Thus, even if *all the paths of the Lord are mercy and truth* [Ps 25:10], this is especially evident at the end when mercy is manifest in the reward of the good and justice in the punishment of the wicked. It is for this reason that the prophet David sings: *Two things have I heard*—namely mercy and justice: *that you repay to each one according to his works* [Ps 62:11-12]. To the good, who possess the merit of grace, he will give the reward of glory, but to the wicked who possess the demerit of sin, the divine justice will render the torment of Gehenna.

The Receptive Subject of Creation: the World, Inner Conscience, and Heaven

Let us now turn to the phrase: *in his field.* This brings us to my second point: the creation of humankind in terms of its receptive subject, designated here by the word "field." As the Lord explains it, in this instance the field signifies the world from which man was formed in regard to his body *of clay* [Gn 2:7]; in regard to his soul, however, he was formed out of nothing. Now in the scripture we find that the word "field" is used to signify the fabric of the world, the inner conscience, and our heavenly homeland. So we have the field of the fabric of the world, the inner conscience, and the heavenly homeland. The field which is the fabric of the world should be disdained as an occasion of wandering and deviancy. The field which is the inner conscience should be cultivated, for it can receive the word of God, but the field which is the heavenly homeland should be desired for the fragrance and the beauty of its divine flower.

First, let us consider why the field of the fabric of this world should be disdained as being a source of wandering and deviancy. Job alludes to this in the passage: *For it*—namely, Behemoth—*the mountains yield food, where all the beasts of the field play* [40:20]. It is because of their inordinate attachment to this mundane field that sinners turn away from God; therefore, their hearts yield the prickly fruits of vice, which Behemoth, that is, the devil, feeds on and delights in. *All the beasts of the field*, namely, the devils lurking in this world, *play* there. They applaud, when through their devious tricks they manage to entice human souls made in the image of God into earthly affections, deterring them from the love of penance with the distraction of vain ideas, alluring them instead with the charm of worldly pleasures. Thus, in the book of Genesis it is said of Joseph: *A man found him wandering in the field* [37:15]. Joseph wandering in the field, whose name is interpreted here as "attachment," stands for the person who attaches his heart to the fleeting delights of the field of the world for love of them, he has wandered away from the path of seeking the kingdom of God, even though it is gratuitous, free of cost, and available to all. The heart of the greedy person strays in this manner, for what is gratuitous, he would make cheap; what is free of cost, something base, and what is available to all, he would appropriate to himself. Because of this deviant error, this worldly field should be disdained, even if we must make use of it to take care of our bodily needs.

Now the second field, that of the inner conscience, should be cultivated so that it might receive the word of God. Proverbs admonishes us: *Diligently till your field* [24:27]. The Wise One goes on to relate in the same passage: *I passed by the field of one who was lazy, by the vineyard of a stupid person; and see, it was all overgrown with thorns; the ground was covered with nettles, and its stone wall was broken down* [24:30-31]. Having observed this, let it serve as an example. The *field* stands for the body; the *vineyard*, the soul. These will become *overgrown with* the *thorns* of vices and the *nettles* of wanton desires unless cultivated through holy discipline and good training. The *stone wall* is *broken down* when the bulwark of virtue is abandoned. So when wise persons see all this, they learn from this example to rid the field of their conscience, indeed of their entire body, from the *thorns* of vices through the good exercise of virtuous conduct and the *nettles* of wanton desires through the discipline of constant mortification. What is written in the prophet Zechariah is thus fulfilled: *The Lord will give to each* year *grass in the field* [10:1].

The third field, that of the heavenly homeland, should be desired for the fragrance and beauty of the divine flower. Indeed, one reads in the psalm: *I know all the birds of the air, and with me is the beauty of the field* [50:11]. This beauty of heavenly glory, which one finds in God the Father, is nothing else than the beauty of all things, sensible and insensible, rational and irrational, of the humanity of Christ and of God one and triune. These are given to the contemplation of the glorified spirit, symbolized by *the birds of the air,* because the wings of contemplation are raised even to union with the heaven where the Trinity resides. From *the beauty of* that *field* such a fragrance emanates that it reaches one's inmost being and intoxicates the whole heavenly court. It was this perfume that the holy Isaac sensed in Jacob when he exclaimed in the spirit of prophecy: *Ah, the smell of my son is like the smell of a field that the Lord has blessed* [Gn 27:27]. Indeed, Christ too was like a field filled with the flowers of virtue, namely with the roses of grace and the lilies of the gifts of the Holy Spirit and the fruits of sweet consolations. It is their fragrance which the contemplative soul experiences when it utters the cry of the Song of Songs: *Come, my beloved, let us go forth into the field* [7:11].

The Intermediate Act of Creation:
Material, Spiritual, and Heavenly Influences

We now have reached our third point: the creation of humankind from the viewpoint of the intermediate act, expressed in the sowing of good seed, for the parable tells us: he *sowed good seed*. Properly speaking, the Creative Power first sowed both spiritual and material substances into the field of the fabric of the world, giving the substratum of natural existence. The Wisdom governing the inner field of the conscience and the soul then sowed heavenly influences, granting the perfected existence of grace. The Goodness drawing all things to their completion finally sowed in the field of the heavenly homeland the everlasting splendors which bestow the fulfilled existence of glory.

First of all, the Creative Power sowed in the field of the fabric of the world both spiritual and material substances, giving the substratum of natural existence. As Jeremiah says: *I planted you as my choice vineyard, all true seed* [2:21]. This *vineyard planted* by almighty God is the world. His *true seed* is humankind, for being fashioned according to the image and likeness of God, it was intended to be seed disposed to the moisture of heavenly rain, sprouting up into the vigor of grace and growing until the mature harvest of glory. An *enemy*, that is, the devil, sowed the false seed of vices and sins in order to suffocate the true seed, so that it might not sprout into the bud of grace. This is what Matthew tells us: *"Master, did you not sow good seed in your field? Where, then, did these weeds come from?" He answered, "An enemy has done this"* [3:27-28].

Then the Wisdom governing the inner field of the conscience, or soul, has sown heavenly influences, granting the perfected existence of grace. Thus Hosea prophesied: *I will sow her for myself in the earth; and I will have mercy on her that was without mercy* [2:23]. God had compassion on erring souls when from them he weeded out all the thorns of vice, sowing instead, as in choice earth, the seed of the word of God, which could sprout into grace and grow until the full harvest of glory.

This is why the Lord also says in Matthew: *But as for what was sown on good soil, this is the one who hears the word and understands it, who indeed bears fruit* [13:23]. The word of God is *sown on good soil* when it is heard with reverence and understood by being put into practice; for it is then that the devout soul, like good soil, *bears* the *fruit* of grace when it carries into action what it has grasped.

Finally, the Goodness which draws creatures to the heavenly field has sown the everlasting splendors which bestow the fulfilled existence of glory. Thus, Isaiah says: *These are the seed whom the Lord has blessed. I will greatly rejoice in the Lord, my soul shall exult in my God; for he has clothed me with the garments of salvation* [61:9-10]. *These are the seed*: namely, the everlasting splendors shining in the presence of the divine beauty. These *the Lord has blessed* with the beatitude of glory. With this immediate vision of the face of God, the glorified soul is seized with such an overwhelming desire to *greatly rejoice* with supreme gladness, both exteriorly, at the sight of the humanity of Christ, and interiorly, *in God,* at the sight of the Godhead. These truly have been *clothed with the garments of salvation.* May the Lord grant that we may be worthy to enter there.

Sermon for Passion Sunday

If someone keeps my word, he will not taste eternal death. [Jn 8:52]

Since it is the duty of a good gardener to uproot a tree that does not produce fruit and throw it out, so that it does not take up space in the garden to no avail, Our Lord Jesus Christ speaks the aforementioned words *If someone,* etc. In this regard he wishes, just like a good gardener, for each tree in his garden, namely, the Church on earth, to bear fruit, so that it would not be cut down by the axe of eternal damnation. Just as there is a certain order in cultivating a tree—first, the tree receives the influence of the sun's rays, then the tree produces a bountiful harvest of fruit, and, thereafter, great care must be taken to ensure that the tree does not perish—so, too, in the manner of its expression there is a certain order in the aforementioned saying of our Lord. First, the saying notes the emanation of the divine ray of goodness in the phrase *my word;* second, the saying notes the bountiful harvest of good work when it joins the former to the phrase *If someone keeps;* third, the saying notes the escape from eternal damnation when it concludes *he will not taste eternal death.*

The Influence of the Word of God on the Soul

First, the emanation of the divine ray is expressed when Jesus says *my word.* Just as a physical tree is disposed through the sun's influence to bring forth good fruits, so too the spiritual tree, that is, the human soul, is disposed through the emanation of the divine and good speech to multiply works of justice and holiness in all of its various powers. Indeed, the divine speech first illuminates the rational power of the soul through the understanding of the truth of the faith, then enkindles the desiring power of the soul through the good will of Christ's love, and finally strengthens the spirited part of the soul through the persevering endurance of hope. When the soul has these three things, namely, faith, hope, and charity, then the soul is well disposed in all of its powers to acting well.

The divine speech first illuminates the rational power of the soul through the understanding of the truth of the faith. This is the reason for what is said in the Psalms: *The expression of your speech brings enlightenment and gives understanding to the little ones. I drew up my spirit and opened my mouth, because I was earnestly seeking to fulfill your commands* [118:130-131]. For if someone wishes to be enlightened by the ray of the divine speech, one must prepare and dispose oneself after the manner of David when he says: *I have opened my mouth*; that is, one should ready oneself, calling upon the divine name in prayer with the earnest desire to pay heed to the divine precepts. There is no better preparation for coming to know the truth than calling upon the divine name in prayer together with steadfast obedience to the divine precepts. *And I drew up my spirit*, says David, through gathering together and returning both the senses and exterior acts to inward things, since *one who lessens his outward activity will perceive true wisdom.* Then will the *expression of your speech*, through its own words giving a clear explanation of the divine eloquence within, enlighten anyone hearing these words without. The understanding of how to put into practice thoroughly what is heard respectfully is given to *the little ones*, not to the proud since the swollen pride of the mind is a stumbling block to understanding the truth. "Pride may build up our spirit, but it also casts a shadow over our minds," as Gregory says in his *Moral Lessons*. John also speaks of the need for preparing the mind to receive the illumination of truth when he says: *If you keep my word, you will truly be my disciples* [8:31]. *You will come to know the truth and the truth will set you free*, that is to say, free from the shadows of ignorance and spiritual blindness. This is why John also says: *Make yourselves holy in the truth since your speech is truth* [17:17].

Secondly, the divine speech enkindles the concupiscible appetite with the goodwill of Christ. Hence, it is said in Proverbs that the *speech of God is a fiery shield for all of those who hope in the divine mercy* [30:5]. The divine speech is, accordingly, *a fiery shield* in the manner of fire, so that it may not grow lukewarm within us by the weakness of fear, and it shields the whole body after the manner of a shield and a breastplate, so that it may not be injured or attacked by any temptation of the devil. Likewise, this same feature of the divine speech is discussed in Hebrews: *Living is the speech of God and powerful and more cutting than a two-headed sword, reaching, indeed, to the division of spirit and body* [4:12].

Thirdly, the divine speech strengthens the irascible appetite with persevering endurance of hope. It is said in the Gospel of Luke: *I shall show you what every person is like who comes to me, hears my words, and does what they say. He is like a man building a house who dug deep into the ground and placed its foundation upon rock. When a flood came, its waters rushed upon the house but could not move it at all; for the house had been founded upon rock* [6:47-48]. Every person who comes to me through faith and *hears my words* with devout attention *and does what they say* through the performance of good works is *like a man*, that is, Christ the Mediator, *building a house*, the Church. The interlinear explanation regards the next words *who dug deep into the ground and places its foundation upon rock* as referring to the basis of the Church not being the changeable character of earthly things but the everlastingness of eternal things. The "Gloss" on this text therefore states: "*He dug deep into the ground* indicates someone who, instructed by the precepts of humility, altogether uproots all earthly things from his heart, so that he may not serve God on account of any changing thing and have a lasting home merely in earthly things." *When the flood came*, that is, when persecution arose, *its waters rushed*, that is, the lust of the flesh, the delights of the world, and the attack of devils; *upon that house*, that is, "the building of the virtues" *and could not move it*, that is, destroy it. The cause of this failure to destroy the Church is that *it was built upon a rock*, that is, Christ: "What falls away is not built upon Christ." A similar statement is made in the Second Book of Maccabees: *He armed each one of them not with the strength of shield and spear, but with his best words* [15:11].

The Harvest of Good Works

There follows after this the words *if someone keeps* where we find some indication of the fruit of good works. To the extent that the soul is enlightened by the influence of the divine speech, enkindled by the charity of Christ, and strengthened by the persevering endurance of hope, it is very well disposed to heeding the divine word. It is from heeding this word that it produces fruit of good works in great abundance. For this reason the soul, acting in accordance with the aforementioned threefold disposition grounded in the influence of the divine word, ought to be fruitful or heed the divine speech, which is tantamount to being fruitful through good works. First, insofar as it is enlightened by the truth of the faith, the soul ought to keep the divine word in the purity of its conscience by scorning the world. Second, insofar as it is enkindled by the goodwill of Christ's charity, it ought to keep the divine speech with the full breadth of goodwill by loving God. Third, if it is strengthened by the persevering endurance of hope, it should keep the divine speech with the strength of patience by enduring evil.

Turning to the first of these points, we may say that the soul should, inasmuch as it is enlightened by the truth of the faith, keep the divine word with a pure conscience by despising the world. This is why we read in John: *I declared your name to those persons whom you gave me from the world; they were yours but you gave them to me and they have kept your word* [17:6]. This saying is in the person of Christ speaking to the Father: *I declared your name to those persons,* that is, to simple and humble ordinary men *the truth that you hid from the wise and astute; whom you gave me from the world* [Mt 11:25] because of the need to keep them pure and clean, which cannot be accomplished in the world. Everything in the world is either the concupiscence of the flesh, which makes people pleasure-seeking and licentious, or the concupiscence of the eyes, which makes them desirous and greedy, or the pride of life, which makes them powerful and seekers of power. *They were yours* through the grace of adoption *but you gave them to me* as my disciples to make them knowledgeable in the way of salvation. This is why God first adopts each person like a son and then hands him over to Christ, or to his representative, as his disciple so that he may learn to scorn earthly things and seek heavenly ones. This is also why the apostles, being cleansed and rendered faultless through their scorning of earthly things and their desire for divine things, kept the divine word in the purity of their consciences, which is needed to keep the divine word.

Second, the soul enkindled by the love of Christ ought to keep the divine word in its love of God with the breadth of good-will. It is said in John: *If someone loves me, he will keep my word and my Father will love him; and we shall come to him and make our dwelling in him* [14:23]. Since the proof of divine love consists in the display of good works, the Lord says: *If someone loves me, he will keep my word;* as if he should say "my love is proved by good works" insofar as "the love of God does great things, if it is truly present; if someone's love refuses to perform great and good things, it is not really the love of God." Our Lord adds: *and my Father will love him*, on account of the keeping of his word; for the fruit of the human obedience or good works is the condescending bestowal of the divine love and tenderness. *And we shall come to him*, this is through the sevenfold gift of divine grace, *and we shall make our dwelling in him,* that is, through the broadcasting and fulfillment of good works. This is why we read in the Book of Wisdom: *Desire then my words and hold them dear, and you shall have discipline* [6:12], this is discipline of fatherly correction, not the sentence of eternal damnation.

Third, strengthened by the persevering endurance of hope, the soul ought to keep the divine speech in enduring evil with the firmness of long suffering. In Revelation it says: *Because you have kept the word of my long suffering, I shall preserve you from the hour of temptation* [3:10]. Someone keeps the word of long suffering who through the model of patience never ceases to heed the divine speech, no matter how many the enticements, condemnations, or insults encountered, which encourage to give up. To such a person, Christ says: *I shall save you from the hour of temptation*; and particularly in the case of death, wherein the devil always tries to tempt human beings in such a way that he may ultimately undermine their salvation. Wherefore Gregory writes in his *Moral Lessons*: "Unless our merciful Lord slightened the trials before us in such a way as to make them proportionate to human powers, no one would be able to avoid the snares of the evil ones."

Freedom From Eternal Death

To return to the main text of John, let us follow closely the meaning of the final phrase *he will not taste eternal death* [8:52]. In this saying we see an indication that if we are faithful we shall experience an escape, or freedom, from eternal death. Yet because no one can be free from the death of the eternal calamity unless he is preserved or freed from the death of his own sinfulness, and likewise it is impossible for someone to be free from that same death unless he first is free from the death of original sin, each mature member of the Church heeding the divine speech undergoes a series of liberations throughout their lives. First, they are freed from the death of original sin through the grace of baptism. Next, they are freed or preserved from the death of their own sinfulness through the grace of penance. Finally, they are freed from the death of eternal punishment through glory which makes them like unto God.

First, then, a member of the Church is freed from the death of original sin through the grace of baptism. We read in Paul's Letter to the Romans: *For as by the sinfulness of one man death entered into human life, all the more will those who receive the abundance of grace, gifts, and justice reign in the eternal life through the one Christ Jesus* [5:17]. For *if by the sinfulness of one man*, our first parent, *death* has ruled in the lives of all others who have descended from that source through the means of lust and sensual desire, *all the more those who receive the abundance of grace* in the kindheartedness of adoption *and gift* in the fullness of the charisms of the Holy Spirit *and justice* in the promotion of good works *will reign in the eternal life* of grace through baptism as heirs and kings of the kingdom of heaven *through the one Christ Jesus.* Here the apostle argues by topical inferential rule "a minori," in that the grace of Christ is much more strong in its goodness than the fault of our first parent was in its evil. This is why, too, we read in the First Letter to the Corinthians: *Just as all die in Adam* by the demerit of his lie, *so too all will live in Christ* through the sacrament of baptism by the merit of his passion [15:22].

Second, a member of the Church is freed from the death of his own sinfulness through the grace of penance. We read in Ephesians: *Those who sleep wake up and rise from the dead, and Christ will enlighten you* [5:14]. *Those who sleep* should *wake up* through despising their own evildoing, *rise* through abandoning their sinful ways *from the dead*, that is, from the deadly deeds committed in mortal sin outside the bounds of charity. Nothing done outside the bounds of charity is worthy of eternal reward. *And Christ will enlighten you* through the pouring forth of the illuminating grace through which we come to know the true difference and distance of good from evil. Our souls know they have wandered from the path of righteousness when they remain steadfast and delight in evil and have scorned the Unchanging Good. We read about this in the Psalms: *Who is the man who will live and will not see death? How will he rescue his soul from the hand of hell?* [88:49]. The answer is: The one who will live by the life of grace, and he will not see the death of his own failings who saves his soul from the hand of hell by practicing the works of penance.

Third, a member of the Church is freed from the death of eternal punishment through the glory which makes him like unto God. We read in the First Letter to the Corinthians: *For it is necessary that this corruptible flesh put on incorruptibility and this mortal nature dons immortality. When moreover this mortal nature has donned immortality, then the saying will be fulfilled which states "death has been swallowed up in victory"* [15:53-54]. *It is necessary* moreover *that this corruptible mortal flesh put on incorruptibility and immortality* through conformity to the purity of Christ's body, Christ who is our head. Otherwise something unfitting would occur: The head would be beautiful and immortal, while the other members of the body would be corruptible and deformed. Once we are conformed to Christ, *death will be swallowed up* in the victory of the resurrection of Christ.

Sermon for the Second Sunday before Lent

But that on the good ground are those who, when they hear the word, hold it fast in a good and honest heart and bring forth fruit with patience. [Lk 8:15]

Give an occasion to the wise, and they will become wiser still. In the words of this second passage taken from the Book of Proverbs [9:9], three things are described which are required of anyone who wishes to propound the word of God. These are a spirit of generosity, brevity in speech, and the prospect of usefulness. A generous spirit is indicated when it says: *Give.* That is, do not sell it for a price or barter it, for the Lord says: *Freely you have received, freely give* [Mt 10:8]. Brevity in speech is alluded to in what follows: *an occasion.* Such an occasion is offered to listeners when, in the words of the Rule of the Friars Minor "a brief discourse, vices and virtues" are proclaimed to them *"because a short word the Lord* made *upon the earth."* The prospect of usefulness is noted when it concludes: *and they will become wiser still.* So, dear friends, let us beseech the Lord at the beginning of this sermon that he might give me a generous spirit and brevity in speech, so that something useful for you might result. Amen.

But that on the good ground are those who, when they hear the word, hold it fast in a good and honest heart and bring forth fruit with patience. According to Saint Gregory in his *Moral Lessons*, "humility discloses to us the light of understanding, pride conceals it." So our Lord Jesus Christ, aware that it was well-pleasing to God the Father, proclaimed the reign of God to proud, haughty, human beings only through parables, so that he might humble the conceited minds of those who heard but did not understand. To his disciples, to whom *it was given to know the mystery of the kingdom of God* [Mt 13:11], he laid open the meaning of the parable in today's gospel when he told them in this passage which concludes his exposition of this parable: *But that on the good ground are those,* etc. Notice that in this parable he proceeds in a very orderly fashion. As we all know, if earthly soil is to yield fruit, first of all it must be prepared, then sown; only afterwards may fruit be gathered from it. So in this passage, we are informed first about the necessary preparation of our hearts; secondly, about the steadfast reception of the divine seed; and thirdly, once the seed has been received, about the fruit which is produced in due season. It alludes to the necessary preparation of the heart in the words: *that on the good ground*, for this goodness of the ground is nothing else than the proper preparation of our heart. Next, it refers to the steadfast reception of the divine seed when it says: *those who, when they hear the word, hold it fast in a good and honest heart*. Finally, it speaks of the received seed bearing fruit in its season when it concludes: *and bring forth fruit with patience*. This refers to those who endure persecution patiently on account of the word of God, and all other kinds of afflictions as well, whether these be caused by others or come from within.

Preparation of the Heart for the Word of God

Let us first examine, then, the necessary preparation of our heart in the passage: *that on the good ground*. We should ready our heart, which Christ here describes through the metaphor of "the good ground," in the same way as material soil. Notice the way in which the earth is well prepared and thus readied to bear fruit: first, it is totally cleared of noxious roots; next, it is irrigated by streams of water; finally, it is exposed to the heat of the sun. Only insofar as it is warmed by the sun's life-giving rays can the sown seed germinate. So we too must proceed in a similar fashion, if indeed we want our heart to be well prepared and readied to produce the fruit of good works: first, we must uproot all the thorny growth of sin; then, we must water it through the tears of contrition; finally, we must be inflamed with holy desires, for only with this life-giving warmth can the received and retained word of God germinate and bear the fruit of good works.

First of all, the noxious roots of sin must be cleared from the soil of our heart. As the Book of Proverbs says: *The one who tills his land shall be satisfied with bread, but the one who follows idleness is very foolish* [12:11]. *The one who tills* the *land* of his own conscience, rooting out the brambles of vice with the sharp spade of contrition, pulling up the thorn bushes of sin by means of a sincere confession, and clearing away the nettles of evil desires through the practice of discipline and mortification, *will be satisfied with* the *bread* of good works. *But the one who follows idleness*, letting his land be overgrown with the brambles of vice, the thorns of sin, and the nettles of evil desires, is *very foolish*. This is why it is good to till your land: *that you might bring forth bread from the earth and wine to cheer the human heart*, as the psalmist says [104:14]. Yes, this is the way for *you to bring forth* the *bread* of good works for your nourishment *from the earth* of your own conscience and the *wine* of inner devotion *to cheer* it.

Next, the soil of our heart must be irrigated by the water of our repentant tears. As it is said in the Book of Judges: *Give me a blessing, for you have given me arid land; give me also basins of water* [1:15]. The devout soul knows from its own experience that an abundant flow of tears and deep contrition of the heart do not come from itself but from God. It is for that reason that it seeks its own healing: *Give me a blessing*, and then I will water the *arid land* of my conscience with the water of the tears of compunction. The psalmist also cries: *My soul thirsts for you like a parched land. Answer me quickly, my spirit fails* [143:6-7]. Zealous David was well aware that his soul, *like a parched land*, could not produce the yield of good works without being watered by tears of contrition and irrigated by inner devotion. So he begged the Lord, imploring fervently: *Answer me quickly*, sending the moisture of interior devotion and external weeping, *for my spirit fails* parched by the lack of inward feeling and by the heat of worldly affections.

Finally, the soil of our heart must be inflamed by a desire for the things of God. As Sirach tells us: *The sun, when it appears, proclaims as it rises, what a marvelous instrument it is, the work of the Most High. At noon it burns up the land* [43:2]. The *sun* of justice, that is, Christ our God is radiant in his divinity when he appears within, just as he was outwardly in his humanity. He is *a marvelous instrument* indeed, containing the incomprehensible Godhead, for *in him the whole fullness of deity dwells bodily* [Col 2:9]. He is called *the work of the Most High*, for even though the Most High Lord forms all things in nature, he has, nonetheless, fashioned Christ in a marvelous way that transcends nature. He truly *at noon burns up the land*, that is, when he sets our heart on fire with a burning love for himself.

The Reception of the Word of God

After this, the passage continues: *these are the ones who, when they hear the word, hold it fast in a good and honest heart.* This refers to the steadfast reception of the divine seed. That we might hear in a way as will bear fruit, today's gospel teaches that we must first receive the word, listening to it reverently with inner tranquillity; second, that we must hold it fast, firmly believing it with total fidelity; and third, that having understood it we must lovingly put it into practice through our deeds.

First of all, we must receive the word of God reverently, listening to it with tranquillity of spirit. Our Lord warns us in today's gospel: *As for what fell among the thorns, these are the ones who hear; but as they go on their way, they are choked by the cares and riches and pleasures of life, and their fruit does not mature* [Lk 8:14]. Gregory tells us in his *Moral Lessons*: "The troubled minds of the worldly cry out by the mere circumstance of their not being quiet, that they are widely separated from true Wisdom." In a similar vein, he says: "We do not learn the secret things of God unless virtuous desires flourish within us; . . . it is then that the mind penetrates, in a more lively manner, the words of God, when it refuses to admit within the tumults of worldly cares." For *the words of the wise are heard in quiet* [Eccl 9:17]. Mary Magdalene recognized this; as Luke tells us, she *sat at the Lord's feet and listened to his word* [10:39]. She *sat* in tranquillity of spirit, not running to and fro with an unsettled heart. As Gregory teaches us in the *Moral Lessons*, the one who seeks wisdom should withdraw from cares and distractions; *only the one who has little business can become wise* [Sir 38:24]. Instead, she *sat at Jesus' feet* with a humble heart, "for the swollen mind is an impediment in the way of truth, because while it puffs us up it obscures our view." Instead, she *listened to his word*, inclining her ear, *forgetting her* Jewish *people, and* her *father's house*, that is, the devil's, whose child she was by performing his works.

Next, we must hold the word fast, firmly believing it with total fidelity. Thus, the Lord refers to those who do not retain it well: *The ones on the rock are those who, when they hear the word, receive it with joy. But these have no root; they believe only for a while and in a time of testing fall away* [Lk 8:13]. Concerning those who firmly believe it, holding it fast, he continues: *But as for that in the good ground, these are the ones who, when they hear the word, hold it fast in a good and honest heart and bear fruit with patience* [Lk 8:15], that is, when they patiently endure persecutions and all other types of evil on account of the word of God.

Finally, having understood the word, we must put it into practice by our deeds, for the Lord warns us about those who listen but fail to do anything about it, saying in Matthew: *When anyone hears the word of the kingdom and does not understand it, the evil one comes and snatches away what is sown in the heart; this is what was sown on the path* [13:19]. He continues, referring to those who put into practice what they have understood: *But as for what was sown on good ground, this the one who hears the word and understands it, who indeed bears fruit, yielding in one case a hundred-fold, in another sixty, and in another thirty* [13:23]. The word is sown on good soil when what is understood is put into practice; then the word *bears fruit thirty-fold* in married folk, *sixty-fold* in the continent, but *a hundred-fold* in virgins. The merit of married folk is designated by the number *thirty*, which is the multiple of 3 and 10; this signifies that married people possess faith in the Trinity and adhere to the ten commandments of the Law. Likewise, the number *sixty*, which is the multiple of 6 and 10, denotes the merit of the continent, inasmuch as they too observe the ten commandments of the Law but also devote themselves to the six works of mercy as expressed in the following verse:

I visit, give drink, feed, redeem, clothe, shelter, bury.

The continent should visit the sick, feed and give drink to the starving, redeem the captive, clothe the naked, house the stranger, and bury the dead. The merit of virgins, because of its perfection, is designated however by the number *a hundred*. Now this hundred and the reason for its perfection may be laid out on your right hand. To explain this statement better, and why the Lord expressed the merits of the third state with this number and not with another, we should not forget what experts in the art of calculating tell us. In this way, we might appreciate just how ingenious and appropriate his assigning these numbers to the various merits is. The number of digits comes from the five fingers of the hand, which those skilled in the art call: the thumb, the index, the middle, the curative [ring], and the ear [little] finger. Now, why they are named in this order I will omit for the sake of brevity. So bend back your ear or little finger and place it on your palm; this signifies 1. When you bend back your ring finger on the palm next to the little finger, together they signify 2. When the finger which is in the middle of the others is positioned in the same way with the other two, this signifies 3. The calculation does not continue in this manner. Instead, when you stand up your little finger, while the ring and middle finger are bent down [on the palm], this stands for 4. When both the little and ring finger are erect, while the middle finger is bent down on the palm, this stands for 5. When the ring finger is bent down, and the middle and little finger are standing up, this denotes 6. Now, when you extend your little finger above the palm, this signifies 7; when you extend your ring finger in the same manner, this stands for 8; the middle finger, 9. Now, when you place the index finger on the middle of your thumb, this signifies 10. When the index finger is placed straight against the thumb, this stands for 20. If you bend it over in such a way that the tip of the index finger touches the tip of the thumb, this signifies 30; fittingly, the Lord chose to express the merit of married folk with this number, as their touching signifies carnal union. Now, when you tightly move the index finger over the thumb to form a cross, this stands for the number 60. It is fitting that this number designates the merit of continent folk, because their life is bent away from carnal pleasures by imposing reason upon their sensuality through the voluntary imposition of the cross. The number 100, which as the perfect number is designated with the full right hand, most appropriately indicates the merit of the virginal state because of its perfection; for virgins lead, insofar as possible, an angelic and heavenly life.

The Fruits of the Word of God

The third thing to note in the text I have selected is that the seed, once received, bears fruit in due season: *and they bring forth fruit with patience.* First, those who have cleared all the briars of sin from their heart and received the word reverently in tranquillity of spirit bear the gorgeous fruit of the purity of beautifying cleanliness. Second, those who have filled their heart with the water of tears of compunction and who have received the word, steadfastly believing it, bear the useful fruit of the clarity which illuminates the understanding. Third, those who have set their heart on fire for the things of God and diligently understood the word by putting it into practice bear the delicious fruit of the beatifying divine companionship. Indeed, is not the best fruit that which is beautiful in appearance, useful in purpose, and delicious to the taste?

First of all, those who have cleared their heart of all the briars of sin, receiving the word reverently with tranquillity of spirit, bear the gorgeous fruit of the purity of beautifying cleanliness. As Proverbs says: *For the purchasing of it is better than the merchandise of silver and gold, and her fruit is the purest* [3:14]. For in their eager desire to gain gold and silver, lustful and greedy people become corrupted, abominable in the sight of God and his angels and even to the demons, whom they resemble in the filthiness of their sin. With the acquisition of the beauty of cleanliness, which consists in the unity of grace and the trinity of the theological virtues—namely faith, hope, and charity—the soul becomes beloved in the sight of God, pleasing to the angels, but terrible to demons. This is why *the purchasing of* purity and of cleanliness *is better than the merchandise of silver and gold*. When through purity of heart the soul begins to produce unblemished fruits acceptable to God, these are said to be "first" or *the purest*. In fact, divine Wisdom so loves the souls which possess this purity and cleanliness, that all their works may be appropriated to it and thus may be called "divine" fruits, as Sirach tells us: *Listen to me, divine fruits, and bud forth like roses planted beside brooks of water* [39:17]. Those who possess this purity and cleanliness of thought, affections, and speech are totally transformed by God into the very form of God with the beauty of grace, being divinized in their desiring, thinking, and speaking. They are called *divine fruits*. Like roses, they neither produce the beauty of purity and cleanliness nor yield the fragrant fruit of inner chastity in their heart or exterior in their body, except with the thorns of the sharp discipline of penance. This is why it tells us: *like roses planted beside the brooks of water*, namely, of the gifts which flow from God, *bud forth* the fruit of light and uprightness in all goodness and truth.

Second, those who have filled their heart with the water of tears of compunction and who have received the word, firmly believing it, bear the useful fruit of that clarity which illumines the understanding. Whence the psalmist says: *His delight is in the law of the Lord, and on his law he meditates day and night. And he shall be like a tree planted by streams of water, which yields its fruit in its season* [1:2-3]. This is why the preacher must apply his will first to the divine law, so that he might practice what he understands; then he can *meditate on his law day and night* in order to instruct others. In this way he *shall be like a tree planted by streams of water*; namely, of divine graces, *which yields its fruit in its season.* Many who bear an alien fruit, not their own, wish to put on the shoulders of others *heavy burdens, hard to bear, but they themselves are unwilling to lift a finger to move them* [Mt 23:4]. Still others bear fruit not *in its season* but before its time, because on their own authority they would first teach others before they themselves learn; therefore, their words, because of their scandal or ignorance or evil behavior, often end up profiting their audience nothing and even bring them into disrepute, "for when one's life is contemptible, his preaching also is despised."

Finally, those who have set their heart on fire with desire for the things of God, and who have diligently understood the word by putting it into practice, bear the delicious fruit of sweet divine companionship. The Song of Songs says: *I sat in his shadow, whom I desired, and his fruit was sweet to my taste* [2:3]: that is, in the shadow of his grace, which cools us from the torrid heat of carnal concupiscence and the ardor of pernicious greed; *his*, namely Christ, *whom I desired.* I have earnestly yearned to sit there with my soul at rest, not running about with a capricious spirit, *for he that is less in action shall receive wisdom* [Sir 38:25]. Then, on account of the delight of his wisdom, *his fruit* shall be *sweet to my taste.*

Francis, Herald of God's Word

The Minor Life of Saint Francis of Assisi, presented in this chapter, is a testimony to the mystery of God's Word made flesh in a privileged herald of the divine. This hagiographical text was not the first attempt to draw meaning from a recounting of the major events of Francis' life. Bonaventure's election as Minister General in 1257 by the friars gathered in Rome for General Chapter coincided with their request for a new biography of Francis of Assisi. Several versions of his life were already in circulation; most prominently those of Thomas of Celano. Commissioned by Pope Gregory IX, Thomas completed *The First Life of Saint Francis* in 1229, *The Second Life of Saint Francis* between 1246-47, and *The Treatise on Miracles* around 1252-53. Another friar, Julian of Speyer, compiled a short biography in verse in 1231 or 1232. This rhythmic rendering of Francis' life, together with an abbreviated version of *The First Life of Saint Francis*, was intended for liturgical prayer. At the General Chapter of Narbonne in 1260 Bonaventure received a mandate from the friars to compile a new biography uniting the earlier recounts of Francis' life into a single text destined for universal distribution.

The result of Bonaventure's work, *The Major Life of Saint Francis of Assisi*, was presented to the General Chapter of Pisa in 1263 and soon supplanted all earlier biographies of the saint. A condensed version for liturgical prayer, entitled *The Minor Life of Saint Francis of Assisi*, was also offered to the friars. Although based primarily on the existing efforts of previous biographers, both *The Major Life of Saint Francis* and *The Minor Life of Saint Francis* provide a personal interpretation to the events surrounding the saint's life. *The Minor Life of Saint Francis of Assisi*, whose succinct lessons lend themselves to personal reflection, provides an insight into how Francis' experience of the divine served as a constant resource for Bonaventure's spiritual development. The following themes exemplified throughout Francis' life find a unique voice in *The Minor Life of Saint Francis*: the centrality of Christ, God as good and most high, the divine presence in the world, the importance of the scriptures, the embrace of poverty, devotion to prayer, and the power of love. The investigation and articulation of these themes in word and deed gave purpose and direction to Bonaventure's life and became the abiding hallmarks of his spirituality.

The Minor Life of Saint Francis

His Conversion

First Lesson

The grace of God, our Savior, has shone forth in these latter days in his servant Francis. *The Father of mercy and light* came to his assistance with such an abundance of delightful blessings that, as it clearly appears in the course of Francis' life, God not only led him out from the darkness of the world into light, but also made him renowned for his merits and the excellence of his virtues. He also showed that he was notably illustrious for the remarkable mysteries of the cross displayed in him. Francis was born in the city of Assisi in the region of the Spoleto valley. First called John by his mother, and then Francis by his father, he held on to the name his father gave him, but did not abandon the meaning of the name given by his mother. In his youthful years he was reared in vain pursuits among the idle sons of men and after some knowledge of the liberal arts was destined for the lucrative business of dealer in wares; yet with the heavenly host presiding over and assisting him, neither did he turn aside to follow the yearnings of the flesh among amoral youth, nor did he *put his trust in money or in treasures* among greedy merchants.

Second Lesson

For God placed a noble-minded compassion for the poor together with kindness and gentleness in the heart of the youthful Francis. Increasing in him from early childhood, it had filled his heart with such kindness that, as an attentive listener to the gospel even then, he proposed to give an alms to everyone who asked him, especially if the petitioner mentioned the love of God. In the fullness of his youth he bound himself to the Lord by a firm promise that, if it were possible, he would never deny those who made their petition for the love of God. Since he did not cease to fulfill so noble a promise until death, he attained forevermore abundant increases in grace and in his love for God. Even though a small flame of the fire of the love of God flourished constantly in his heart, as a young man involved with worldly concerns, he was unacquainted with the mystery of the heavenly calling. When the hand of God touched him, he was chastened exteriorly by a long and severe illness and enlightened interiorly by the anointing of the Holy Spirit.

Third Lesson

After Francis' bodily strength was somehow renewed and his mental attitude changed for the better, he had an unexpected meeting with a soldier who was of noble birth but poor in possessions. He was reminded of Christ, the poor and noble king. He was moved toward this man with such compassion that he removed the fine garments which he had just acquired for himself and immediately dressed the soldier, leaving himself without clothes. While he was sleeping the following night, Christ, for the love of whom he had assisted the needy soldier, showed him in a worthy revelation a large and spacious palace with military weapons marked with the sign of the cross. He promised with earnest certitude that everything Francis saw would belong to him and to his soldiers, if he constantly bore the standard of the cross of Christ. From that time on he withdrew from the bustle of public business and sought places suitable for penance in which he would turn his attention unceasingly to indescribable groanings. After a long period of prayer during which he begged the Lord that the way to perfection be shown to him, he merited that his prayer be heard.

Fourth Lesson

One day while he was praying in solitude, Christ Jesus, affixed to his cross, appeared to him and repeated for him so efficaciously this passage of the gospel: *If anyone wishes to come after me, let him deny himself, and take up his cross, and follow me* [Mt

16:24]. Inwardly, this both kindled his heart with the fire of love and filled it with the painfulness of compassion. His soul melted away at the sight of this vision, and the memory of Christ was impressed so deeply on the innermost parts of his heart that with the eyes of his mind he continually, as it were, discerned interiorly the wounds of his crucified Lord and exteriorly was hardly able to repress his tearful laments. When now for the love of Christ Jesus *he despised all the goods of his house* by considering them *as nothing*, he felt that he had found the *hidden treasure* and the brilliant *pearl* of great price. Moved by the desire to possess it, he arranged to leave all his possessions, and by a divine method of commerce he exchanged the business of the world for the business of the gospel.

Fifth Lesson

One day when he went out to meditate in a field, he passed by the church of San Damiano, which because of its great age was on the verge of falling into ruins. Inspired by the Holy Spirit, he entered this church to pray. Prostrate before the image of the Crucified, he was filled in his prayer with a good measure of pleasing consolation. When his tearful eyes were intent on the cross of his Lord he heard in a marvelous way with his bodily ears a voice from the cross, saying to him three times: "Francis, go, repair my church which, as you see, is being totally destroyed!" At the wonderful suggestion of this astonishing voice the man of God first was indeed thoroughly terrified, then filled with joy and admiration. He arose immediately and committed himself totally to the carrying out of the command about repairing the material church; however, the principal intention of the voice referred to that Church which Christ acquired by the precious barter of his own blood, just as the Holy Spirit instructed him, and as he revealed later to his close companions.

Sixth Lesson

Soon afterwards Francis, for the love of Christ, put aside all the things he could and offered money to the poor priest of that church for the repair of his church and for the use of the poor. He humbly asked the priest to permit him to live there for a short time. The priest agreed to let him stay, but for fear of Francis' parents he refused the money. But Francis, now a true despiser of money, cast a large number of coins through a window, demonstrating by this action that he valued as dust what he threw away. Hearing that this had enraged his father, he waited for the anger to pass and hid himself for some days in a dark cave where he fasted, prayed and wept. Finally, filled with a spiritual joy and *clothed with power from on high*, he confidently came forth from the cave and calmly entered the city. When the young people saw his dirty face and changed attitude, they thought that he had taken leave of his senses. They considered him a fool. They threw mud from the street and shouted insulting words at him. But this servant of God was certainly neither broken nor changed by this affront. He passed through it all as though he were deaf.

Seventh Lesson

His father, raging and fuming because of all this, seemed as if he were forgetful of natural compassion. He began to torment with beatings and chains the son who had been dragged home. By wearing down Francis' body with physical abuse, he hoped to turn his mind to the attractions of the world. Finally Francis' father learned by experience that this servant of God was most willing to bear any harsh treatment for Christ and that he could not restrain him. He began to insist vehemently that Francis go with him to the bishop of the city and renounce into the bishop's hands his hereditary right to all his father's property. The servant of the Lord was determined to carry this out further, and as soon as he came before the bishop he did not delay or hesitate or speak or listen to a word. He took off all his clothing instead and, in the presence of those standing around him, discarded even his undergarments. Intoxicated in spirit, he was not afraid to stand naked out of love for him who for us hung naked on the cross.

Eighth Lesson

Now that this despiser of the world was set loose from the bonds of earthly desires, he left the city. While free and without a care, he was singing praises to the Lord in French in the middle of woods when robbers came upon him. As the herald of the great King he was not afraid nor did he stop singing, inasmuch as a half-nude and penniless wayfarer he, like the apostles, rejoiced in tribulation. Then as a lover of total humility he gave himself to the service of lepers, so that while he was subjecting himself to miserable and outcast people under the yoke of servitude, he could first learn perfect contempt of himself and of the world before he would teach it to others. Surely, since he used to fear lepers more than any other group of people, grace was given to him in more abundance. He gave himself up to their service with such a humble heart that he washed their feet, bound up their sores, drew out the festering, and washed off the bloody matter. In an excess of unheard of fervor, he would fall down to kiss their ulcerous sores, putting his mouth to the dust, so that, *filled with reproaches*, he might efficaciously subject the pride of the flesh to the *law of the spirit* and, once the enemy within him was subdued, possess peaceful dominion over himself.

Ninth Lesson

Thereafter, Francis was confirmed in the humility of Christ and made rich in his poverty. Even though he possessed absolutely nothing, he, nevertheless, began to turn his careful attention to repairing the church according to the command given to him from the cross. Although his body was weakened by fasting and bore the burdens of the stone, he did not shrink from earnestly begging the help of alms even from those among whom he had been accustomed to live as a rich man. With the devoted help of the faithful, who now began to realize the remarkable virtue this man of God possessed, he restored not only the church of San Damiano, but also the abandoned and ruined churches of the Prince of the Apostles and of the glorious Virgin. He mysteriously foreshadowed, by an exteriorly perceptible work, what the

Lord disposed to do spiritually through him in the future. For according to the likeness of the threefold buildings repaired under the guidance of the holy man himself, the Church was to be renewed in three ways according to the form, regulation, and teaching of Christ. The voice from the cross, which repeated three times the command concerning the repairing of the house of God, stands out as a prophetic sign. We recognize now that it is fulfilled in the three Orders instituted by Francis.

The Institution of His Order and the Efficacy of His Preaching

First Lesson

After the work on the three churches was finished, Francis stayed at the church dedicated to the Virgin. By the merits and prayers of her who gave birth to the price of our salvation, he merited to find the way of perfection through the spirit of evangelical truth infused into him by God. One day during the solemnity of the mass, that part of the gospel was read in which the evangelical norm for living was prescribed for the disciples who were sent to preach; namely, *do not keep gold, or silver, or money in your girdles, no wallet for your journey, nor two tunics nor sandals, nor staff* [Mt 10:9-10]. Francis, hearing such words, was soon anointed and adorned by the Spirit of Christ with such power that it transformed him into the described manner of living, not only in mind and heart, but also in life and dress. He immediately took off his shoes, threw away his staff, and discarded his purse and its money. He was content with one little tunic; he rejected his leather belt and took a piece of rope for his belt. He applied all the concern of his heart to how he could accomplish what he had heard and adjust himself in all things to the apostolic rule of righteousness.

Second Lesson

Inflamed totally by the fiery vigor of the Spirit of Christ, he began, as another Elias, to be a zealous emulator of truth. He also began to lead some to perfect righteousness and still others to penance. His words were neither empty nor ridiculous; they were, instead, full of the power of the Holy Spirit, and they penetrated to the bottom of the heart. They filled his listeners with great amazement, and their powerful efficacy softened the minds of the obstinate. As his holy and sublime purpose became known among the multitude through the reality of his simple teaching and of his life, some began to be moved to penitence by his example. After they left all things, they joined him in dress and in way of life. That humble man, Francis, decided that they should be called "Friars Minor."

Third Lesson

When at the calling of God the number of friars reached six, their devoted father and shepherd found a place for solitude where, in bitterness of heart, he deplored his life as youth, which he had not lived without sin. He also begged for pardon and grace for himself and for his offspring, which he had begotten in Christ. When an excessive joy filled his being, he became certain concerning the full remission *to the last penny* of all his debt. Then, caught up in ecstasy and absorbed totally in a vivifying light, he saw clearly what the future held for him and his friars. He disclosed this later in confidence for the encouragement of his little flock, when he foretold the Order would soon expand and grow through the clemency of God. After a very few days had passed, certain others joined him, and their number increased to twelve. This servant of the Lord arranged, therefore, to approach the presence of the Apostolic See. Together with that band of simple men, he wished to beg earnestly and humbly that the way of life, shown to him by the Lord and written down by him in a few words, be confirmed by the full authority of that same most Holy See.

Fourth Lesson

Francis, according to his decision, hurried with his companions to come before the presence of the Supreme Pontiff, Lord Innocent III. Christ, the power and wisdom of God, arrived in his clemency before Francis. By means of a vision, it was communicated to the Vicar that he should agree to listen calmly to this poor little suppliant and give him a favorable assent. For in a dream the Roman Pontiff himself saw that the Lateran basilica was at the point of collapsing, and a poor little ordinary man was holding it up by pressing his back against it lest it fall. While the wise bishop was contemplating the purity of the simple mind in this servant of God, his contempt of the world, his love of poverty, the constancy of his perfect proposal, his zeal for souls, and the enkindled fervor of his will, he said: "Truly, this is he who will uphold the Church of Christ by his work and teaching." As a result, the pope from that time on held a special devotion toward this man. Favorably disposed to his petition in all things, the pope approved the Rule, gave him the mandate to preach penance, conceded everything he asked for then, and promised generously to concede more in the future.

Fifth Lesson

Supported then by grace from on high and by the authority of the Supreme Pontiff, Francis with great confidence took the road toward the valley of Spoleto. He wanted to teach by word and carry out by deed the reality of the evangelical perfection which he had conceived in his mind and solemnly vowed to profess. When the question was raised with his companions whether they ought to live among people or seek out solitary places, he sought the will of God through constancy in prayer. Illuminated by a divine revelation, he understood that he was sent by God for the purpose of gaining the souls for Christ which the devil was trying to snatch away. Realizing, therefore, that he was chosen to live more for others than for himself alone, he went to an abandoned hut near Assisi to live with his friars according to the norm of holy poverty in every hardship of religious life, and preach the word of God to the people whenever and wherever possible. Having been made a herald of the gospel, he traveled around the cities and towns announcing the kingdom of God not in such *words as human wis-*

dom teaches, but in the power of the Spirit with the Lord directing him by revelations as he spoke *and confirming the preaching by the signs that followed.*

Sixth Lesson

Once, as was his custom, he was spending the night in prayer apart from his sons. Around midnight, while some of them were sleeping and others were praying, a fiery chariot of remarkable splendor came through the little door of the friars' dwelling. Over this chariot, which turned here and there three times throughout the room, there rested a bright ball of light, which resembled the sun. Those who were awake were stunned at this remarkable brilliant sight. Those who were asleep were aroused and terrified. They experienced a brightness of heart as well as body since, in virtue of this remarkable light, their hearts were laid bare to one another. With one accord, they all understood, since in the hearts of each one they saw each other, that it was their Holy Father Francis who had been transfigured in such an image. Shown to them by the Lord as one *coming in the spirit and power of Elias,* and *as Israel's chariot and charioteer,* he had been made leader of his spiritual army. When the holy man rejoined his friars, he began to comfort them concerning the vision they had been shown from heaven, explore the secrets of their consciences, predict the future, and radiate with miracles. In this manner, he revealed that the twofold spirit of Elias rested upon him in such plenitude that it was perfectly safe for all to follow his life and teaching.

Seventh Lesson

At that time a Religious of the Order of the Cruciferi, whose name was Moricus, was suffering from an illness so serious and so prolonged in a hospital near Assisi that it was believed that he was very close to death. Through a messenger he solicited the man of God, earnestly asking Francis to be willing to intercede for him with God. The holy man kindly assented to his request. After first praying, Francis took crumbs of bread and then mixed them with oil from a lamp which was burning before the altar of the Virgin. He then sent this so-called pastry to the sick man through the hands of his friars as he said: "Take this medicine to our brother Moricus. By means of it the power of Christ will not only restore him to full health, but also will join him forever to our company as a mighty warrior." As soon as the sick man tasted that remedy which had been prepared through the ingenuity of the Holy Spirit, Moricus arose healthy. He had received from God such strength of mind and body that shortly afterwards he entered the Order of the holy man. For a long period of time, he wore a corset of thongs next to his skin, and was content with only raw food. He neither drank wine nor tasted anything that was cooked.

Eighth Lesson

At that time there was a priest from Assisi, whose name was Silvester, who was certainly a man of an honest way of life and possessed dovelike simplicity. In a dream he saw that whole region encompassed by a huge dragon whose loathsome and frightful image, it seemed, threatened imminent destruction to different areas of the world. After this, he saw a glittering cross of gold issuing from Francis' mouth. The top of the cross reached the heavens. Its arms, stretched wide, seemed to extend to the ends of the earth, and the glittering sight of it put that loathsome and frightful dragon to flight forever. While this vision was being shown to Silvester for the third time, this pious man, who was devoted to God, understood that Francis was destined by the Lord to take up the standard of the glorious cross, to shatter the power of the evil dragon, and to enlighten the minds of the faithful with the glorious and splendid truths of both life and teaching. Not long after he gave an account of all this to Francis and his friars, Silvester left the world. In accord with the example of his blessed father, he followed in the footsteps of Christ so perserveringly that his life in the Order proved that the vision which he had while in the world was authentic.

Ninth Lesson

When he was still living the secular life, a certain friar whose name was Pacificus found the servant of God at San Severino, where he was preaching in a monastery. The hand of the Lord came upon him, and he saw Francis marked after the manner of the cross with, as it were, two glittering crossed swords, one of which extended from his head to his feet, and the other across his chest from hand to hand. He did not recognize the man from his appearance, but the miracle revealed who it was. He was exceedingly amazed, frightened, and goaded by the power of Francis' words. Transfixed as it were by a spiritual sword coming from his mouth, he completely despised worldly vanity and joined himself to his blessed father by profession. Afterwards, Pacificus made progress in every moral aspect of religious life. Before he became minister in France, as indeed he was the first to exercise the office of minister there, he merited to see a large Tau on the forehead of Francis which, decorated with a variety of colors, gave a remarkable beauty to his features. Indeed it was with great affection that the man of God venerated this sign of the cross. He frequently recommended it in his speech and used it at the beginning of any action. In those letters which out of charity he sent, he made this mark at the bottom with his own hand. It was as if his whole desire was to conform to the prophetic dictum by making the *Tau upon the foreheads of the men that sign and mourn*, who have been truly converted to Christ Jesus.

The Sure Sign of Virtue

First Lesson

As a loyal follower of the crucified Jesus, Francis, that man of God, crucified his flesh with its passions and desires from the very beginning of his conversion with such rigid discipline, and checked his sensual impulses according to such a strict law of moderation, that he would scarcely partake of the things necessary to sustain life. When he was in good health he hardly and rarely would allow himself cooked food. When he did, however, he made the food bitter by either mixing ashes with it or made it as tasteless as possible by pouring water over it. Withdrawing his flesh from wine in order to turn his mind to the light of wisdom, he preserved such strict control over drinking that when he was suffering from a burning thirst, he hardly would dare to drink enough cold water to satisfy himself. He often used the bare ground as a bed for his wearied body, a stone or a piece of wood for his pillow. The clothes covering him were simple, wrinkled, and rough. Established experience had taught him that malignant spirits are put to flight by using things difficult and harsh, but they are more strongly animated to tempting by things luxurious and delicate.

Second Lesson

Rigid in his discipline, Francis kept an exceedingly attentive watch over himself. He took particular care in guarding the priceless treasure in a vessel of clay, that is, chastity, which he strove to possess in holiness and honor through the virtuous purity of body and spirit. For this reason, around the beginning of his conversion during the winter cold, he would plunge himself many times, strong and fervid in spirit, into a ditch filled with ice or snow. He did this to gain perfect control over the enemy within and to preserve the white robe of purity from the heat of sensual pleasure. Practices such as these enabled him to use his bodily senses in an appealing, modest manner. His mastery over the flesh was now so complete that he seemed *to have made a covenant with his eyes*; he would not only flee far away from carnal sights, but also totally avoid even the curious glance at anything vain.

Third Lesson

Truly, even though Francis had attained purity of heart and body, and in some manner was approaching the height of sanctification, he did not cease to purify the eyes of his spirit with tears. He longed for the sheer brilliance of the heavenly light and disregarded the loss of his bodily eyes. After he incurred a very serious weakness of the eyes due to his continual weeping, a doctor advised him to abstain from tears if he wished to escape the loss of corporeal vision. Francis, however, would not assent to this. He asserted that he preferred to lose the light of bodily vision than repress the devotion of the spirit and impede the tears by which the inner eyes are cleansed in order to see God. He was a man devoted to God, who, drenched in spiritual tears, displayed a serenity in both mind and face. The luster of a pure conscience anointed him with such joy that his mind was forever caught up in God, and he rejoiced at all times in the works of his hands.

Fourth Lesson

Humility, that guard and ornament of all virtues, had by right so influenced the man of God that, although a manifold privilege of virtues was reflected in him, nevertheless, it sought its special domain in him as though in the least of the lesser ones. In his own estimation, by which he accounted himself the greatest of sinners, he was really nothing more than some dirty earthen vessel, while in reality he was an elect vessel of sanctification, set apart by sanctity and glittering with the adornment of many kinds of virtue and grace. Moreover, he strove to be worthless in his own eyes and in those of others, to reveal by public confession his hidden faults, and to keep the Giver's gifts hidden in the secrecy of his heart. He did this so that he would in no way be subject to praise, which could be an occasion for his downfall. Certainly, in order that he might fulfill all justice regarding perfect humility, he so strove to subject himself not only to superiors but even to inferiors that he was accustomed to promise obedience even to his companion on a journey, no matter how simple he was. As a result, he did not give orders as a prelate with authority. In his humility, he would rather obey those subject to him as their minister and servant.

Fifth Lesson

This perfect follower of Christ strove with such undying love to espouse poverty, the companion of humility, to himself that he not only left his father and mother for her but also gave away everything that he was able to possess. No one was so desirous of gold as he was of poverty; nor was anyone more solicitous in guarding of a treasure than he was of the treasure of the gospel pearl. Since from the beginning of his religious life to his death he was rich only in a tunic, a cord, and a pair of undergarments, it would seem that he gloried in want and rejoiced in need. If at any time he saw anyone whose outer garments were poorer than his, he would admonish himself immediately and urge himself to be like him. It seemed as if he were contending with a rival and feared that he would be conquered by the spiritual nobility of that man. Since the pledge of his eternal inheritance, he had preferred poverty to everything perishable, counting as nothing deceptive riches, which are granted to us as a loan for a short time. He loved poverty more than great wealth, and he, who had been taught by poverty to consider himself inferior to everyone, hoped to surpass all in its practice.

Sixth Lesson

Through the love of the most sublime poverty, the man of God prospered and grew rich in holy simplicity. Although he certainly possessed nothing of his own in this world, he seemed to possess all good things in the very Author of this world. With the steady gaze of a dove, that is, the simple application and pure consideration of the mind, he referred all things to the supreme Artisan and recognized, loved, and praised their Maker in all things. It came to pass, by a heavenly gift of kindness, that Francis possessed all things in God and God in all things. In consideration of the primal origin of all things, Francis would call all creatures, however insignificant, by the names of brother and sister, since they come forth with him from the one source. He embraced those, however, more tenderly and passionately, who portray by a natural likeness the gracious gentleness of Christ and exemplify it in the scriptures. It came to pass by a supernatural influx of power that the nature of brute animals was moved in some gracious manner toward him. Even inanimate things obeyed his command, as if this same holy man, so simple and upright, had already returned to the state of innocence.

Seventh Lesson

The source of mercy pervaded the servant of the Lord with such fullness and abundance that he seemed to possess a mother's heart for relieving the misery of suffering people. He possessed an innate kindness which the piety of Christ, poured out upon him, intensified. His soul would melt away at the sight of the sick and the poor, and he would offer his affection to those to whom he was unable to offer a helping hand. With the tenderness of a pious heart, he referred to Christ anyone he saw in need or deprivation. Since he saw the likeness of Christ in all the poor, if any of the necessities of life were given to him, he would not only give them freely to the poor, but he would also think that they should be returned to the poor as if these necessities were their property. He would spare nothing; neither mantles, tunics, books, nor altar cloths. When he could, he gave away all these things to the needy, since he wished to fulfill the duty of perfect love, even *to the utter privation of himself.*

Eighth Lesson

His zeal for fraternal salvation, which emerged from the furnace of love, pierced the inmost parts of this man like a sharp and flaming sword. Aflame with the ardor of imitation and stricken with the sorrow of compassion, this man seemed to be completely consumed. Whenever he became aware that souls redeemed by the precious blood of Jesus Christ were tainted by any stain of sin, he would be pierced by a remarkable sting of sorrow. He would deplore it with such a tender compassion that, like a mother, he would give birth to them daily in Christ. For this reason, he struggled to pray, was active in preaching, and outstanding in giving good example. He did not think that he was a friend of Christ unless he cherished the souls which Christ redeemed. Although his innocent flesh subjected itself freely to his spirit, it had no need of the lash due to offenses. Nevertheless, for the sake of example, he kept on subjecting it to pain and burdens, *keeping the difficult ways* because of others, so that he perfectly followed the footsteps of him *who in death handed over his life* for the salvation of others.

Ninth Lesson

Given the fervor of the perfect love which carried the friend of the Spouse into God, one is able to perceive that he thoroughly desired to offer himself to his Lord as a *living sacrifice* through the sufferings of martyrdom. It was for this reason that he attempted on three occasions to journey to the territory of the infidel. Twice he was restrained by the will of God. On the third attempt, after much abuse, many chains, floggings, and innumerable hardships, he was led with the help of God into the presence of the Sultan of Babylon. He preached Jesus with such an efficacious *demonstration of spirit and of power* that the Sultan was astonished and became docile by the will of God and granted Francis a kind audience. Recognizing in Francis a fervor of spirit, a constancy of mind, a contempt for this present life, and the efficacy of God's word, the Sultan conceived such a devotion toward him that he deemed him worthy of great honor. He offered him costly gifts and earnestly invited Francis to prolong his stay with him. This true despiser of himself and of the world spurned as dirt all that was offered to him. When he realized that he was not able to accomplish his goal after he had truly done all that he could to obtain it, he made his way back to Christian lands as a revelation had suggested. So it was that this friend of Christ with all his strength sought death for his sake and yet by no means found it. Francis did not lack the merit of his desired martyrdom, and he was preserved to be marked in the future with a unique privilege.

His Zeal for Prayer and His Spirit of Prophecy

First Lesson

This servant of Christ felt *exiled* in body *from the Lord*. While his love for Christ had made him totally insensible to all earthly desires, he strove to make his spirit present to God by constant prayer lest he should be deprived of the consolation of his Beloved. Whether walking or sitting, whether inside or outside, whether working or at rest, he was by the power of his mind so intent on prayer that he seemed to have dedicated to God whatever was in him, not only of heart and body, but also of work and time. He was suspended often by such an excess of devotion that, rapt above himself and experiencing something beyond human feeling, he did not know at all what was going on around him.

Second Lesson

That he might receive the infusion of spiritual consolations more quietly, he went at night to pray in solitary places or abandoned churches. However, even there he experienced the horrible assaults of demons who, fighting as it were hand to hand with him, tried to turn him away from his pursuit of prayer. After these demons fled from the unrelenting power of his prayers, the man of God, remaining alone and at peace, filled the groves with his sighs, sprinkled the locality with his tears, and beat his breast with his hand. As if having found a more secret place, he would now respond to his Judge, now implore his Father, now play with his Spouse, now speak with his Friend. There he was seen praying at night with his hands and arms extended in the form of a cross, his whole body lifted up from the ground and surrounded by a glowing little cloud. This extraordinary purification of his body, together with its elevation, was the witness to a marvelous representation and elevation within his soul.

Third Lesson

By the supernatural power of such ecstatic experiences, as has been established by particular evidence, the *uncertain and hidden things of* divine *Wisdom* were open to him. He did not make them known to others except inasmuch as his zeal for fraternal welfare urged him and the impulse of heavenly inspiration forced him. His tireless zeal for prayer together with his continual practice of the virtues had in fact led the man of God to a great clarity of mind. Although he did not possess the learned knowledge of the sacred scriptures which comes through study, nevertheless, illuminated by the splendor of eternal light, he explored the profound things of scripture with a clear, intellectual acumen. The manifold spirit of the prophets also rested upon him with a plenitude of various graces. By its wonderful power, the man of God was present to others who were absent, had certain knowledge of those far distant, saw the secrets of hearts, and also foretold future events, as the evidence of many examples prove, some of which are included below.

Fourth Lesson

At one time the holy man, Anthony, then an eminent preacher but now a famous confessor of Christ, was preaching eloquently to the friars at a Provincial Chapter at Arles on the title of the cross: *Jesus of Nazareth, king of the Jews.* The man of God, Francis, who at that time was busy faraway, appeared elevated in the air at the door of the Chapter. With his hands extended as if in the form of the cross blessing the friars, he filled their spirits with such manifold consolation that their interior spirits testified with certainty that this wonderful apparition had been endowed by the power of heaven. Furthermore, that this did not lie hidden from the blessed Father is evidently clear in how open his spirit would have been to the light of eternal Wisdom, *which is more active than all active things, and reaches everywhere by reason of her purity. She makes her way into holy souls and forms the friends of God and prophets.*

Fifth Lesson

At one time when the friars were entering the Chapter according to custom at Saint Mary of the Portiuncula, one of them, covered with the cloak of an excuse, was not submitting himself to discipline. The holy man of God, who was then praying in his cell as a mediator between those same friars and God, saw all this in spirit. He had one of the friars called to him and said: "Brother, on the back of that disobedient friar, I saw the devil who was holding and squeezing his neck. Constrained by such a rider and having spurned the reins of obedience, the friar was being impelled to follow the devil's reins. Go, therefore, and tell this friar to submit without delay to the yoke of obedience, because he, at whose earnestness in prayer this demon left in confusion, suggests that this be done." The friar, warned by the messenger, perceived the light of truth and conceived the spirit of compunction. He fell forward on his face before the vicar of the holy man, recognized that he was culpable, sought pardon, accepted and bore the discipline, and from then on humbly obeyed in all things.

Sixth Lesson

When Francis was living alone in a cell on Mount La Verna, one of his companions had a great desire to have some brief writing with the words of the Lord from Francis' own hand. This companion was being plagued by a serious temptation, not of the flesh but of the spirit, and he believed that from this writing he would either avoid the temptation or certainly bear it more easily. Wearied by this desire, he was made interiorly uneasy, because since he was humble, modest, and simple, he was overcome by shame and did not dare to disclose all this to his revered Father. The Holy Spirit, however, revealed to Francis what a person did not tell him. He ordered this friar to bring ink and paper to him and, writing the praises of the Lord together with his own blessing in his own hand according to the friar's desire, he graciously gave the friar what he had written, and the entire temptation vanished immediately. This little note, preserved for posterity, brought healing to a great number of people. This made it clear to all how much merit before God this writer had, whose writing left such efficacious power in a small leaf of paper.

Seventh Lesson

At another time, a noble woman, devoted to God, went confidently to the holy man and implored him with all her strength to intercede with the Lord on behalf of her husband, so that his hard heart might be softened by a plentiful infusion of grace. The husband was very cruel to her and opposed her service of Christ. After listening to her, the holy and pious man confirmed her in her good intention with holy words, assured her that consolation would shortly be hers, and finally ordered her to declare to her husband on behalf of God and of himself that now is the time for clemency; later it will be the time for justice. The woman put her trust in the words which the servant of the Lord had spoken to her, accepted his blessing, and in haste returned home. There she met her husband and told him about the conversation she had with Francis, and without any doubt, she waited for the hoped-for promise to be fulfilled. Without any delay, as soon as Francis' words reached his ears, the spirit of grace fell upon him and softened his heart in such a way that from that time on he permitted his devoted wife to serve God freely and offered himself to serve the Lord with her. At the urging of the holy wife, they lived a celibate life for many years and then departed to the Lord on the same day; she in the morning as a *morning sacrifice*, and he in the evening as an *evening sacrifice*.

Eighth Lesson

At the time when the servant of the Lord was lying ill at Rieti, a certain canon named Gedeon, who was deceitful and worldly, was seized with a serious illness. Lying on a stretcher he was brought to Francis, and with tears in his eyes he, together with the bystanders, asked that Francis bless him with the sign of the cross. Francis said to him: "Since you once lived according to the desires of the flesh and not in fear of the judgment of God, I will sign you with the sign of the cross. This is not for your own sake but because of the devout petitions of those interceding for you. I do this with the provision that I let you know, from this moment on, that certainly you will suffer more serious things if, when you are free, you return to your vomit." After the sign of the cross was made from his head to his feet, the bones of his loins resounded and it sounded to all as though dry wood was being broken by hand. Immediately, he who had been lying there constricted arose cured and, bursting forth in praise of God, said: "I have been freed." Then a short time elapsed when, forgetful of God, he returned his body to impurity, and on a certain evening dined in the lodging of a canon and slept there that night. The roof of the house collapsed suddenly on all but killed only him, while all the others escaped death. In this one event it was made manifest how strict is God's zeal for justice with ungrateful people, and how true and certain was the spirit of prophecy which had filled Francis.

Ninth Lesson

At that time after his return from overseas, Francis went to Celano to preach. A soldier with humble devotion invited him to dinner and with great persistence forced him, as it were, to come. Before they began to eat, the devout Francis, who according to his custom offered praise and prayers to God, saw in spirit that this man's judgment was imminent. Francis stood there, lifted up in spirit, with his eyes raised to heaven. Finally, when he completed his prayer, he drew his kind host aside, predicted that his death was near, admonished him to confess his sins, and encouraged him to do as much good as he could. The soldier agreed to what blessed Francis had said, and in confession he revealed all his sins to Francis' associate, put his household in order, committed himself to the mercy of God, and prepared as much as he could to accept death. While the others were taking refreshment for their bodies, the soldier, who seemed strong and healthy, suddenly breathed out his spirit according to the word of the man of God. Even though this soldier was carried off by a sudden death, nevertheless he was so fortified by the weapons of repentance through Francis' spirit of prophecy that he escaped eternal damnation, and according to the promise of the gospel entered into everlasting dwellings.

The Obedience of Creatures and Divine Condescension

First Lesson

Surely, the Spirit of God who had anointed him, as well as *Christ the power and the wisdom of God* was with his servant, Francis. It was this grace and power that brought it about that not only did uncertain and hidden things become evident to him, but even the elements of this world obeyed him. At one time doctors advised him, and the friars earnestly exhorted him, to allow his eye affliction to be healed by cauterization. The man of God humbly assented, because this would not only be a remedy for a bodily weakness but also a means for practicing virtue. Given the sensitivity of the flesh, he cringed with an instinctive horror at the sight of the still-glowing iron. The man of God addressed the fire as a brother, admonishing it in the name and in the power of its Creator to temper its heat that he might be strong enough to bear its gentle burning. When the crackling iron was placed on his tender flesh and the burning brand was drawn from his ear to his eyelash, the man filled with God exulted in spirit and said to his friars: "Praise the Most High, because I confess what is true; neither the heat of the fire troubled me, nor did pain in the flesh afflict me."

Second Lesson

While the servant of God was laboring under a very serious illness at the hermitage of Saint Urban, he felt a natural weakness. He asked for a drink of wine but was told that there was no wine there to give him. He then ordered water to be brought to him, and, with the sign of the cross, he blessed it. What had been pure water immediately became the best of wine, and what the poverty of this deserted place could not produce, the purity of this holy man attained. At the taste of it, he became well with such ease that it became evidently clear that the desired "drink" was given to him by a bountiful Giver not as much to please his sense of taste as to be efficacious for his health.

Third Lesson

At another time, the man of God wished to go to a certain hermitage that he might occupy his time more freely in contemplation. He was carried on an ass belonging to a poor man, because he was in a weakened condition. While this man followed the servant of God and climbed into mountainous country on a hot day, he became very tired from the journey over a rather rough and long road. When he became faint from an exceedingly burning thirst, he began to shout insistently and say that unless he had a little something to drink, he would die immediately. The man of God dismounted from the ass without delay, knelt on the ground, raised his hands to heaven, and did not cease praying until he felt his prayer was heard. When he finally finished his prayer, he said to the man: "Hurry to that rock, and there you will find running water, which Christ in his mercy has produced from a rock for you to drink at this time." The thirsty man ran to the place pointed out to him and drank the water produced from the rock by the power of a praying man, and he consumed the drink furnished for him by God from solid rock.

Fourth Lesson

At one time, when the servant of God was preaching near the sea at Gaeta, he wished to escape the adulation of the crowd, which in its devotion was rushing toward him. He jumped alone into a small boat, which was close to the shore. The boat, as though it were guided by an internal source of power, moved itself rather far from land without an oarsman. All who were present saw this and marveled. After the boat moved a moderate distance over the sea into the deep, it stopped immobile among the waves until, with the crowd waiting on the shore, it pleased the man of God to preach. After they listened to the sermon, witnessed the miracle and received the blessing they asked for, the crowd moved away. By the influence of no other command but a heavenly one, the boat reached the shore; it subjugated itself without rebellion, as if it were a creature zealously *serving its Maker*, to the perfect worshipper of the Creator and obeyed him without hesitation.

Fifth Lesson

At one time when Francis was staying in the hermitage of Greccio, the inhabitants of that place were burdened by many calamities. Every year a hailstorm devastated the annual harvest and the vineyards, while a large number of ravenous wolves devoured not only animals but people as well. The servant of the all powerful Lord was filled with a benevolent compassion for those sorely afflicted people. In a public sermon, he personally promised and guaranteed them that the entire pestilence would vanish if they would confess their sins and be willing to produce worthy fruits of penance. From the very time that the people began doing penance at Francis' exhortation the devastation ceased, the dangers disappeared, and neither the wolves nor the hail caused any trouble. What is greater still, in fact, is that if a hailstorm ever passed through the cultivated fields of neighboring areas and approached the boundaries of these people, it would either end there or be diverted to another area.

Sixth Lesson

At another time the man of God was journeying around the valley of Spoleto in order to preach. As he was approaching

Bevagna, he came to a place where a very large flock of birds of different kinds had congregated. Looking at them with affection, the Spirit of the Lord came upon him, and he hurriedly ran to the place, eagerly greeted them, and commanded them to be silent, so that they might attentively listen to the word of God. While he recounted many things about the benefits of God to these creatures, who were gathered together, and about the praises that should be returned to him by them, they began to gesture in a remarkable manner; they extended their necks, stretched out their wings, opened their beaks, and looked attentively at him, as if they were trying to experience the marvelous power of his words. It was only proper that this man, full of the spirit of God, was led by a humane and tender affection to such irrational creatures. For their part, those birds were drawn to Francis so remarkably that they listened to him when he was instructing them, obeyed him when he commanded them, flocked to him without fear when he bid them welcome, and, without distress, remained with him.

Seventh Lesson

When Francis had tried to go overseas to pursue the palm of martyrdom, he was impeded by storms at sea from accomplishing his purpose. The Director of all things remained with him to such an extent that his providence snatched him, together with many others, from the dangers of death and showed forth his wonderful works on his behalf in the depths of the sea. When he was proposing to return from Dalmatia to Italy and had boarded a ship without any provisions at all, a man sent from God came, as Francis stepped aboard, with necessary provisions for Christ's little poor man. Then this man gave the provisions to a God-fearing man whom he called from the ship, that he might administer them at the proper time to those who had absolutely nothing. Since the sailors were never able to bring the ship to shore due to the force of the wind, all their food was consumed. All that remained was a small portion of the alms which had been given from above to the blessed man. Because of his prayers, merits and the power of heaven, these alms increased so much that for many days, as the storm at sea continued, they took complete care of everyone's needs until the ship reached the desired port of Ancona.

Eighth Lesson

At another time when the man of God was on a preaching journey with a friar companion between Lombardy and the Marches of Treviso, the darkness of night overtook them near the Po river. Since the road would be exposed to many great dangers because of the river, the marshes, and the darkness, his companion insisted that in this necessity Francis should implore divine assistance. The man of God replied with great confidence: "God is powerful. If it is agreeable with him, he will make light for us by putting the darkness of night to flight." What followed was marvelous! He had hardly finished speaking when, behold, by the power of God such a great light began to radiate around them that, while the darkness of night remained in other places, they saw in clear light not only the road but also many other things on the other side of the river.

Ninth Lesson

The brightness of heavenly splendor went before them amid the dense darkness of the night in a fitting manner indeed. This proved that those who follow the light of life on a straight path are not able to be overwhelmed by the shadow of death. Guided in body and comforted in spirit by the remarkable splendor of such a light, they arrived at a hospice singing hymns and praises to the Lord after traveling a good distance along the road. He was a truly outstanding and admirable man, for whom fire tempers its burning heat, water changes its taste, a rock provides abundant drink, inanimate things obey, wild animals become tame, and to whom irrational creatures direct their attention eagerly. In his benevolence the Lord of all things listens to his prayer, as in his liberality he provides food, gives guidance by the brightness of light, so that every creature is subservient to him as a man of extraordinary sanctity, and even the Creator himself condescends to him.

The Sacred Stigmata

First Lesson

The truly faithful servant and minister of Christ, Francis, two years before he would give up his spirit to heaven, began a forty day fast in honor of the Archangel Michael in an isolated, elevated location called Mount La Verna. Steeped more than usual in the sweetness of heavenly contemplation and inflamed by a more ardent fire of heavenly desires, he began to experience a greater abundance of the gifts sent to him from God. The seraphic ardor of desires raised him into God, as he was transformed by the compassionate tenderness of affections into him who was pleased, with a love beyond measure, to be crucified. While he was praying one morning on the side of the mountain around the Feast of the Exaltation of the Holy Cross, he saw the likeness of a Seraph, which had six fiery and glittering wings, descending from the heights of the heavens. He came in swift flight to a place in the air close to the man of God. The Seraph not only appeared to have wings but also to be crucified. His hands and feet were extended and fastened to a cross, and his wings were arranged on both sides in such a remarkable manner that he elevated two above his head, extended two for flying, and with the two others he encompassed and covered his whole body.

Second Lesson

When he saw this, Francis was thoroughly and deeply astonished. His mind was filled with a rush of joy mixed with sorrow. He experienced an incomparable joy in the pleasing vision of Christ, which appeared to him so wonderful and intimate, while the deplorable sight of being affixed to a cross pierced his soul with the sword of compassionate sorrow. He understood, as the one whom he saw exteriorly taught him interiorly, that the weakness of suffering by no means befits the immortality of a seraphic spirit; nevertheless, such a vision had been presented to his sight, so that this friend of Christ might know beforehand that he had to be transformed totally, not by a martyrdom of the flesh but by the fervor of his spirit, into the manifest likeness of Christ Jesus crucified. The vision, which disappeared after a secret and intimate conversation, inflamed him interiorly with a seraphic ardor and marked his flesh exteriorly with a likeness conformed to the Crucified; it was as if the liquefying power of fire preceded the impression of the seal.

Third Lesson

Nail marks began to appear immediately in his hands and feet. Their heads appeared on the inside of the hands and on the top of the feet and the pointed parts on the opposite sides. The heads of the nails in his hands and feet were round, and their points, which were hammered and bent back, emerged and stood out from the flesh. The bent part of the nails on the bottom of his feet were so prominent and extended so far out that they did not allow the sole of his feet to touch the ground. In fact, the finger of a hand could be put easily into the curved loop of the points, as I heard from those who saw them with their own eyes. His right side also appeared as though it were pierced with a lance. It was covered with a red scar, which often shed his holy blood. His tunic and undergarments were soaked with such a quantity of blood that his friar-companions, when they washed these clothes, undoubtedly observed that the servant of the Lord had the impressed likeness of the Crucified in his side as well as in his hands and feet.

Fourth Lesson

The man, filled with God, realized that the stigmata, which was impressed so splendidly on his flesh, could not be hidden from his intimate companions; nevertheless, he feared making this secret of the Lord public. He was put into a great agony of doubt as to whether he should tell what he had seen or keep silent. Forced by the sting of conscience, he finally related with great fear the sequence of the vision to some of the friars who were closer to him. He added that he who appeared to him told him other things, which he would never reveal to any person as long as he lived. After the true love of Christ *transformed* the lover into the *image of the beloved,* Francis' forty days on that mountain of solitude were completed and the solemnity of the Archangel Michael was at hand. The angelic man, Francis, came down from the mountain bearing the likeness of the Crucified, not sketched by the hand of an artist on tablets of stone or wood, but *etched* on his fleshy limbs by the *finger of the living God.*

Fifth Lesson

This holy and humble man tried afterwards with all diligence to conceal these sacred marks; nevertheless, it pleased the Lord to display through them certain marvelous things for his glory. Their hidden power, therefore, could be made manifest by clear signs and irradiate like a bright star amid the dense darkness of a darkened age. Before the holy man spent time around Mount La Verna, for example, a dark cloud would arise from the mountain and a violent hail storm regularly devastated the fruits of the earth. After that providential vision, the customary hail ceased to the admiration and joy of the inhabitants. The very aspect of the sky, tranquil beyond usual, proclaimed the supreme worth of that vision from heaven and the power of the stigmata impressed there.

Sixth Lesson

At that time a very serious disease swept through the province of Rieti and began to afflict the sheep and the oxen to such an extent that almost all of them seemed to languish under an incurable illness. A God-fearing man was admonished by a vision one night to hurry to the friars' hermitage where the blessed Father was then staying and request from his companions the water he used to wash his hands and feet. He was then to sprinkle this water on the suffering animals and thereby put the pestilence to an end. After the man diligently completed this task, God gave great power to the water which had touched the sacred wounds. Even a little of the water completely drove out the plague from the suffering animals it touched. Once they recovered their pristine vigor, they ran to their fodder as though they had experienced no previous misfortune.

Seventh Lesson

Finally, from that time on, those hands attained such marvelous power that their saving touch returned both robust health to the sick and living sensation to limbs now dry and paralytic. What is greater, they restored unimpaired life to those who had been mortally wounded. I will anticipate and recall briefly to mind for you two of Francis' many miracles. Once at Lerida, a man, whose name was John and who was devoted to blessed Francis, was so cut and savagely wounded one night that one could hardly believe that he would survive until the next day. Our holy Father appeared marvelously to him and with his sacred hands touched those wounds. At the very same hour John was so restored to full health that all the region proclaimed that this wonderful standard bearer of the cross was most worthy of all veneration. Who would not be surprised to look upon a person he knew well who, at almost the same moment of time, was mangled by the most cruel wounds and then rejoiced in unimpaired health? Who would be able to recall this without giving thanks? Finally, who could ponder in a spirit of faith such a tender, virtuous, and remarkable miracle without experiencing devotion?

Eighth Lesson

At Potenza, a city of Apulia, a cleric named Roger was thinking foolish things about the sacred stigmata of our blessed Father. He received a blow to his left hand under his glove, as though from an arrow shot from a bow. His glove, however, remained untouched. He was subject to the sting of excruciating pain for three days. Feeling remorseful, he called upon and entreated blessed Francis earnestly to help him by means of those glorious stigmata. He received such perfect health that all the pain disappeared and not a trace of a blow remained. From this it seems perfectly clear that those sacred marks of his were impressed by a power and provided with the strength of him whose characteristic it is to inflict wounds, to provide remedies, to strike the obstinate, and *to heal the contrite*.

Ninth Lesson

This blessed man certainly appeared worthy to be marked with this singular privilege, since his whole endeavor, both public and private, centered around the cross of the Lord. What else than his wonderful gentleness, the austerity of his life, his profound humility, his prompt obedience, his extreme poverty, his unimpaired chastity; what else than the bitterness of his compunction, his flow of tears, his heartfelt compassion, his zeal for emulation, his desire for martyrdom, his outstanding charity, and finally the privilege of the many virtues that made him Christ-like: What else stood out in him than these similarities to Christ, these preparations for the sacred stigmata? For this reason, the whole course of his life, from the time of his conversion, was adorned with the remarkable mysteries of the cross of Christ. Finally, at the sight of the sublime Seraph and the humble Crucified, he was transformed totally by a fiery, divine power into the likeness of the form which he saw. Those who saw them, touched them, kissed them testified to this; and after having touched these most sacred wounds, they confirmed them with greater certitude by swearing that they saw them and that they were exactly as reported.

Francis' Death

First Lesson

The man of God was now nailed with Christ, in both body and spirit, to the cross. Just as he was being raised up into God by the fire of seraphic love, he was also being transfixed by a fervid zeal for souls. He thirsted with his crucified Lord for the deliverance of all those in need of salvation. Since he was not able to walk due to the nails growing out on his feet, he had his dried up body carried around the towns and villages, so that like *another angel ascending from the rising of the sun*, he might kindle the hearts of the servants of God with a divine flame of fire, direct their feet into the way of peace, and seal their foreheads with the sign of the living God. He also was burning with a great desire to return to the beginnings of his humility, so that he might, just as he did in the beginning, minister to lepers and recall his body, now failing due to hardships, to its original servitude.

Second Lesson

With Christ as his leader, he proposed to do great things, and though his limbs were becoming weak, he was strong and fervid in spirit, and he hoped for a victory over his enemy in a new encounter. Surely, in order that there might be an increase in the sum total of merits, which truly makes everything perfect by patience, the little one of Christ began to be burdened seriously by various infirmities. The painful agony of suffering was diffused throughout his limbs, his flesh was being consumed, and it seemed that only skin was clinging to his bones. While he was being tormented by unyielding pains, he said that those punishing conditions were not *pains* but *his sisters*. He gave such praise and thanks to the Lord in the joyful bearing of them, that it seemed to the friars taking care of him that they were looking upon Paul in his joyful and humble glorying, and that they were seeing another Job in the vigor of his imperturbable spirit.

Third Lesson

Francis knew the time of his passing long before his death. As this day was approaching, he told his friars that the tent of his body had to be laid aside very soon, as it had been pointed out to him by Christ. Two years after the impression of the sacred stigmata and in the twentieth year of his conversion, he begged to be brought to Saint Mary of the Portiuncula. He wished to pay his debt to death and arrive at the prize of eternal recompense there where he had conceived the spirit of perfection and grace through the Virgin Mother of God. After he was brought to the Portiuncula, he demonstrated by a true example that there was nothing in common between him and the world. During that illness which was so serious that it ended every weakness, he placed himself in total nudity on the ground, so that in his last hour when he still could be angry, he might wrestle naked with his naked enemy. Lying thus on the ground and in the dust, this nude athlete covered with his left hand the wound in his right side, lest it be seen. With his serene face raised in the customary manner toward heaven and his attention directed entirely toward that glory, he began to praise the Most High because, released from all things, he was now free to go to him.

Fourth Lesson

Finally, with the hour of his passing now imminent, he had all the friars living in the area called to him. Consoling them in preparation for his death with comforting words, he exhorted them with fatherly affection to the love of God. Then leaving them their rightful inheritance, the possession of poverty and peace, he charged them to strive toward things eternal and fortify themselves against the dangers of this world. He carefully admonished them and persuaded them with all the efficacy of speech he could muster to follow perfectly the footsteps of Jesus crucified. As his sons were sitting around him, the patriarch of the poor, whose eyes had been dimmed not by age but by tears, the holy man, blind and now near death, crossed his arms and extended his hands over them in the form of the cross, because he always loved this sign. He then blessed all the friars, both present and absent, in the name and in power of the Crucified.

Fifth Lesson

After this, Francis begged that the Gospel according to John be read to him beginning with the words: *Before the feast of the Passover*. He wished to hear the voice of the Beloved knocking, from whom only the wall of flesh now separated him. Finally, when all the mysteries were completed in him, the blessed man, praying and singing psalms, fell asleep in the Lord. His most holy soul, free from the flesh, was absorbed in the abyss of eternal splendor. At that very hour one of his friars and disciples, a man certainly famous for his sanctity, saw that fortunate soul in the likeness of a brilliant star, borne up by a little cloud over many waters straight into heaven. This soul, glittering with the clear luster of his conscience and glistening with the sure sign of his merits, was being raised on high so effectually by an abundance of graces and divine virtues that nothing would be able to detain it at all from its vision of heavenly light and glory.

Sixth Lesson

The minister of the friars at that time in Terra di Lavoro was Augustine, a man who was certainly dear to God and close to death. For a long time he had been without the power of speech, but now he called out to those listening who were standing by and said: "Wait for me, Father, wait! Look, I am coming with you!" To the friars who wondered and asked to whom he was speaking, he asserted that he saw blessed Francis going into heaven. As soon as he said this, he also happily went to his rest. At the same time the bishop of Assisi had gone to the Oratory of Saint Michael at Monte Gargano. Blessed Francis, filled with delight, appeared to him in the hour of his passing, and said that he was leaving the world and passing exultantly into heaven. Arising in the morning, the bishop told his companions what he saw. Then, after returning to Assisi and making careful inquiries, he found out for certain that the blessed Father had departed from this life at the same hour in which it was made known to him in a vision.

Seventh Lesson

The immensity of celestial goodness deigned to show, by many prodigies and miracles after his death, just how remarkable this man was for his outstanding sanctity. Because of his merits and at his intercession the power of almighty God restored sight to the blind, hearing to the deaf, speech to the mute, walking to the lame, and feeling and movement to the paralyzed; he gave robust health, moreover, to those who were withered, shriveled or ruptured, and effectually snatched away those who were in prison; he brought the shipwrecked to the safety of port, granted an easy delivery to those in danger during childbirth, and put demons to flight from those possessed. Finally, he restored those hemorrhaging and lepers to wholesome cleanliness, those mortally wounded to a perfectly sound condition, and, what is greater than all these, he restored the dead to life.

Eighth Lesson

Because of him innumerable benefits from God do not cease to abound in different parts of the world, as even I myself who wrote the above have experienced in my own life. When I was just a child and very seriously ill, my mother made a vow on my behalf to the blessed Father Francis. I was snatched from the very jaws of death and restored to the vigor of a healthy life. Since I hold this vividly in my memory, I now publicly proclaim it as true, lest keeping silent about such a benefit I would be accused of being ungrateful. Accept, therefore, blessed Father, my thanks however meager and unequal to your merits and benefits. As you accept our desires, excuse too our faults through prayer, so that you may both rescue those faithfully devoted to you from present evils and lead them to everlasting blessings.

Ninth Lesson

It is fitting, therefore, that these words be concluded with a brief recapitulation of everything that has been written. Whoever has read thoroughly the things above should ponder carefully these final considerations: the conversion of the blessed Father Francis which took place in a marvelous way; his efficacy in preaching the word of God; his privilege of exalted virtues; his spirit of prophecy together with his understanding of the scriptures; the obedience shown to him by irrational creatures; the impression of the sacred stigmata; and his celebrated passage from this world to heaven. These seven testimonies clearly attest and show to the whole world that he, the herald of Christ, *having the seal of the living God*, should be venerated by reason of his accomplishments, and for the fact that he was authentic in his teaching and admirable in his sanctity. So let those who *are leaving Egypt* feel secure in following him. With the *sea divided* by the staff of the cross of Christ, *they will traverse the desert* and crossing the Jordan of mortality they will enter, by the wonderful power of that cross, *into the promised land of the living*. Through the prayers of our blessed Father may they, there, be conducted to that glorious Savior and leader Christ to whom with the Father and the Holy Spirit in perfect Trinity be all praise, honor, and glory forever. Amen.

Christ, God's Incarnate and Eternal Word

Bonaventure lived during a period of intense renewal manifested in the widespread attempts of lay and religious men and women to pattern their lives on the portrait of Christ depicted in the gospels. While some wandered beyond the then acceptable bounds of ecclesial teaching and tradition, others like Francis and Clare of Assisi managed to receive papal approbation without sacrificing their original dynamism. Regardless of their status in the medieval Church, these men and women were united in the desire for evangelical authenticity as they interpreted the world through the prism of Christ's life. In his writings, Francis looks repeatedly to the life of Christ mirrored in the gospels and speaks of him as the Word of God. He offers a broad vision of Christ, which focuses on his humanity without losing sight of his eternal divinity. In the paradoxical language of poverty and power, Christ is perceived as divine in the indigence of birth, the privation of begging, the pain of crucifixion and the humility of the eucharistic encounter. Francis' efforts to enter into the mystery of Christ, evidenced in the example of his life as well as writings, encouraged Bonaventure to articulate the centrality of Christ's life in the spiritual journey.

Bonaventure often drew insights from gospel events to illustrate how the careful consideration of Christ's life is key to understanding the fundamentals of spiritual discernment and growth. The first work in this chapter, *The Five Feasts of the Child Jesus*, is an example of what was to become a popular genre of spiritual writing in the Middle Ages. Bonaventure outlines in heartfelt language how prayerful reflection on the birth and childhood of the divine infant is an ideal way to conceive the Word of God within the recesses of the soul. The second work in this chapter, *Christ, The One Teacher of All*, does not highlight any one event in Christ's life as much as the importance of being united with him whose humanity and divinity reveals the Way, the Truth, and the Life. The centrality of Christ in the spiritual journey is expressed in Bonaventure's belief in him as the only teacher who, as the incarnate and eternal Word, stands as mediator between humanity and God.

The Five Feasts of the Child Jesus

In God's Church there are holy men and women who have been enlightened more profoundly than others by divine radiance and inflamed more ardently by inspiration from on high. It is their conviction and teaching that through meditation upon Jesus and reverent contemplation of the incarnate Word, a faithful soul can experience a delight far sweeter, a pleasure more thrilling, and a consolation more perfect than from honey and fragrant perfumes.

I had the opportunity to withdraw for a short while from the turmoil of distracting thoughts. In my innermost self I asked which aspect of the Lord's incarnation should be the object of my reflection during this time. My purpose was to obtain some spiritual consolation in which I might savor the divine sweetness reflected, as in a mirror, *in this vale of tears* [Ps 83:7], and, having savored it, however fleetingly, to keep myself more resolutely from passing any illusory consolations.

As I considered these things, it arose mysteriously in my mind that by the grace of the Holy Spirit and the power of the Most High, a soul dedicated to God could spiritually conceive the holy Word of God and only-begotten Son of the Father, give birth to him, name him, seek and adore him with the Magi, and finally, according to the law of Moses, joyfully present him in the Temple to God the Father. In this way, as a true disciple of the Christian faith, a soul would be able to celebrate with all prayerfulness and piety the five feasts of the Child Jesus, which the Church has instituted.

Because I thought out this little work with humility, I have written it in simple words, and for brevity's sake, I have omitted references to authorities confirming what I have said.

Should anyone grow but a little in devotion toward our most sweet Jesus, from reading or meditating on this short and modest work, then let him praise, glorify, and bless the Author, Fount, and Origin of all goodness. If no such growth takes place, then let the reader either blame me for not having written it well or worthily enough or perhaps, for lack of devotion and humility on his part, blame himself.

The First Feast
How Christ Jesus, the Son of God, May Be Conceived Spiritually by a Devout Soul

Our understanding has to be purified by the waters of sorrow, our heart inflamed and raised on high by the gentle fire of love. Then by fervent meditation and prayerful thought, we can undertake our first consideration: How it is that the blessed Son of God, Christ Jesus, may be conceived spiritually in a devout soul.

Once a devout soul has been touched or moved by the hope of heavenly bliss, the fear of eternal punishment, or the weariness of living long *in this vale of tears* [Ps 83:7], it is visited by fresh inspirations, set alight with holy desires, and taken up with godly thoughts. When at length it has rejected and despised previous imperfections and former desires for worldly things, and has resolved to lead a new life by the gracious kindness of *the Father of lights* from whom is *every good endowment and every perfect gift* [Jas 1:17], it conceives mystically by the gift of grace.

What is happening here? It is nothing other than the heavenly Father impregnating the soul, as it were, and making it fruitful by a divine seed. *The power of the Most High comes* upon the soul and *overshadows* it [Lk 1:35] with a heavenly coolness, which tempers the desires of the flesh and gives help and strength to the eyes of the spirit.

It is a joyous conception which leads to such contempt of the world and to such longing for heavenly works and the things of God. No matter how fleetingly up to this point, even in the midst of distress, the things of the spirit have been tasted, the things of the flesh lose their savor.

Now, with Mary, the soul begins to climb *the hill country* [Lk 1:39], because after this conception earthly things lose their attraction, and the soul longs for heavenly and eternal things. The soul begins to flee the company of those *with minds set on earthly things* [Phil 3:19] and desires the friendship of those with hearts set on heavenly things. It begins to take care of Elizabeth, that is, to look to those who are enlightened by divine wisdom and ardently inflamed by love.

There is an important point to keep in mind because it applies to many people: The further one withdraws from the world, the closer becomes one's friendship with good people. It follows that the more the company of ungodly people loses its attraction, the more the company of saintly and spiritual people inspires the heart with radiant delight. Saint Gregory says: "Anyone who keeps close to a holy man discovers that by seeing him often, listening to his words and witnessing his exemplary behavior, he is set on fire with love of the truth, keeps away from the darkness of sin, and is inflamed by the love of divine light." Saint Isidore writes: "Seek the company of good people. If you share their company, you will also share their virtue."

The faithful soul should consider well how pure, holy and devout was the conversation of the saints, how godly and salutary their counsel, how admirable their holiness, and all they achieved to their mutual benefit, as they inspired one another by word and example toward greater virtue.

Devout soul, that is also what you should do when you realize that you have, by the Holy Spirit, conceived a new longing for the life of grace. Avoid the company of the wicked, go up into the hill country with Mary, seek the advice of spiritual people, strive to follow in the footsteps of the saints, reflect upon the teaching of holy people and also upon their actions and example. Keep clear of the poisonous counsels of the wicked, who always try to distort new desires inspired by the Holy Spirit and want to hinder them and never cease to tear them to shreds.

Often under the guise of holiness they infect the soul with the contagion of an insidious cowardice. They say such things as: "What you have begun is beyond you; what you are taking on is far too difficult; what you are doing is too much of a burden. Your strength is not up to it, you do not have the ability to do it. Your mind will get confused, your eyesight will be destroyed, you will develop all kinds of illnesses: consumption, paralysis, stones in the kidneys, dizziness in the head, dulling of the senses, clouding of the mind, and loss of faculties. All these terrible things will happen to you if you do not abandon what you have started and take greater care of your health. Such practices do not become your position, they harm your honor and good name."

You notice then how someone can masquerade as a master of discipline and a medical doctor who does not even know how to keep his own life in order or cure the sickness of his own mind! How sad it is that the cursed advice of the worldly-minded has frequently ruined so many people and killed the Son of God conceived in them by the Holy Spirit. This is that damnable and deadly medicine, the devil's counsel, which hinders spiritual conception in so many souls and kills and destroys in many others what had been conceived by a firm decision or a vow.

There are others who seem to be good, religious people, and perhaps they are, but who, I say it with respect, are far too timid. They neither remember that *the hand of the Lord is not yet shortened that it cannot save* [Is 59:1], nor do they remember that the kindness of the Most High has not yet run out, that he wants to help us and has the power to do so. *They have a zeal for God but it is not enlightened* [Rom 10:2]. Out of compassion for physical suffering or perhaps from fear of natural weakness, they dissuade others from the pursuit of perfection. That is their reaction when they see others achieving successfully that which they themselves had judged to be good and holy, but upon which they did not have the courage to embark. They discourage others from anything that goes beyond the common average, and they destroy the salutary counsels which come from God's inspiration. The more authentic these counsels are in the light of their experience, the more dangerous they find them to be.

Sometimes through the cunning of the ancient enemy, they slyly suggest: "If you take on such and such practices of piety, people will say you are holy, good, devout, and religious. Because you have not yet acquired the virtues which others think you have, you will be judged guilty in the sight of the Supreme Judge, who knows in all their horror your great and terrible sins. You will forfeit the merits of your good works, and you will be judged a liar and a hypocrite." Such practices of piety, they maintain, are only for those who have not sinned gravely and have kept to a chaste and holy life, who gave up everything for God and have remained faithful to him all their lives.

Beloved soul dedicated to God, keep clear of people like that. *Go up into the hill country* [Lk 1:39] with Mary. Paul did not live a sinless life, yet he had not been in God's service for any length of time when he was taken up into the third heaven and contemplated God face to face. Mary Magdalene had been full of pride and ambition, totally intent on worldly vanities and ensnared by the pleasures of the flesh. Not long after her conversion, however, she sat among the holy apostles at the feet of Jesus and listened attentively to the saving doctrine of perfection. She was found worthy to be the first to see the Lord shortly after his resurrection, and she proclaimed steadfastly to the others that he was risen from the dead.

God shows no partiality [Acts 10:34]. He does not take account of nobility of birth, length of time in his service, or the number of our good works. What counts with God is a devout soul's increased fervor and more ardent love. He does not consider how you once behaved, but what you have now begun to be. You see, therefore, how gravely blameworthy the advice of such would be, did ignorance not excuse it, though it cannot be condoned.

If then you cannot be saved through innocence, strive for salvation by penance. If you cannot be a Catherine or a Cecilia, do not be ashamed to be a Mary Magdalene or a Mary of

Egypt. If you recognize that you have conceived God's most dear Son by a sacred resolve to strive for perfection, then keep away from the deadly poison I have just mentioned, and like a woman in labor, hasten with desire and longing toward a happy delivery.

The Second Feast
How the Son of God Is Born
Spiritually in a Devout Soul

Secondly, let us consider and mark well how the blessed Son of God, already conceived spiritually, is born spiritually in the soul. He is born when, after good advice, due thought and prayer for God's protection, we put into practice our resolution to lead a more perfect life. That is to say, he is born when the soul begins to do that which it long had in mind but was afraid to undertake through fear of its own weakness. The angels rejoice at this most blessed birth, they glorify God and announce peace.

They announce peace because peace is restored to the soul by the practice of the virtues which it long had in mind. God's peace cannot be established firmly in the soul while the spirit and flesh are at war with one another; when the spirit longs for solitude and the flesh craves to be with the crowd; when the spirit delights in Christ and the flesh is allured by the world; when the spirit seeks the serenity of contemplation in God and the flesh desires positions of honor in the world.

On the other hand, when the flesh is subjected to the spirit, that is, once good works are put into practice—which for so long the flesh had hindered—inner peace and joy are restored to the soul. How happy a birth which brings such rejoicing to human beings and angels! How lovely and delightful it would be if we always did what was best for us. But our foolishness prevents it. Once we rid ourselves of our foolishness, human nature recognizes what is native to it. In this birth we experience the truth of that gospel saying: *Take my yoke upon you, and learn from me, for I am gentle and lowly in heart, and you will find rest for your souls. For my yoke is easy and my burden is light* [Mt 11:29-30].

Devout soul, if this happy birth brings you delight, you should remember that you have to be like Mary. The name "Mary" means "'bitter sea," "one who enlightens" and "one who rules." First, you must be a "bitter sea" through tears of sorrow, weeping bitterly for the sins you have committed, lamenting deeply the good you left undone, and reproaching yourself unceasingly for the time you let slip by and lost. Second, you must be "one who enlightens" by speaking words of edification, practicing virtue and teaching others untiringly to do good. Third, you must be "one who rules," that is, be master of your senses, carnal passions, and all your actions. In this way all your actions will be in conformity with right reason, and in all that you do you will seek and long for God's praise and glory, your neighbor's edification, and your own salvation.

How blessed is such a "Mary" who weeps over sins committed, shines resplendently with virtue and has complete mastery over all carnal desires. Jesus Christ does not disdain to be born spiritually and joyfully, without pain and sorrow, from a "Mary" like this.

Once this birth has taken place, the devout soul knows and tastes how good the Lord [Ps 34:9] Jesus is. In truth we find how good he is when we nourish him with our prayers, bathe him in the waters of our warm and loving tears, wrap him in the spotless swaddling clothes of our desires, carry him in an embrace of holy love, kiss him over and over again with heartfelt longings and cherish him in the bosom of our inmost heart.

That is how this Child is born spiritually in a devout soul.

The Third Feast
How the Infant Jesus Is Named
Spiritually by a Devout Soul

Thirdly, we come to consider how this holy Infant, now born spiritually, shall be named. I think there is no name more fitting for him than Jesus, for scripture says: *He was called Jesus* [Lk 2:21]. This is the most sacred of all names. It was foretold by the prophets, announced by an angel, proclaimed by the apostles, and desired by all the saints. O powerful name! O grace-filled and joyous name! O delightful and glorious name!

This name is *powerful,* because it brings down our enemies, restores our strength, and renews our mind. It is *grace-filled*, because in it is contained the foundation of faith, the ground of hope, and the fulfillment of holiness. It is *joyous,* because it is gladness to the heart, music to the ear, honey to the tongue, and splendor to the mind. It is *delightful,* because it nourishes when it is recalled, soothes when it is uttered, anoints when it is invoked, refreshes when it is written, and instructs when it is read. It is a truly *glorious* name, because it gives sight to the blind, makes the lame walk, brings hearing to the deaf, speech to the dumb, and life to the dead. O blest name endowed with such powers!

Devout soul, whether you are writing, reading, or teaching or whatever you are doing—may nothing have taste for you, nothing please you, apart from Jesus. To the little Infant begotten in you spiritually, give the name Jesus, which means: Savior, amidst the miseries of this life. May he save you from the vanities of the world which entice you, from the deceits of the devil which surround you, and from the weakness of the flesh which torments you.

Devout soul, amidst the many scourges of this life cry out:

Jesus, Savior of the world, save us
   whom you have redeemed by your cross
   and blood.
Help us, O Lord our God.

Save us, sweet Jesus, our Savior.
Strengthen the weak, comfort those who mourn,
help the frail and give constancy to the
    faint-hearted.

After this holy name had been given to the Child, the Virgin Mary, fruitful mother in the flesh and true mother in the spirit, often felt a sense of sweetness when through this name she witnessed that devils were cast out, miracles were performed, the blind received their sight, the sick were restored to health and the dead were brought back to life.

Undoubtedly you also, devout soul, as spiritual mother of this Child, have every right to rejoice and give praise, as you witness in yourself and in others that your holy Son, Jesus, *casts out devils* in the remission of sins; *gives sight to the blind* by infusing true knowledge into the mind; *raises the dead* through the gift of grace; *cures the sick, heals the lame* and *restores the paralyzed and crippled* by giving strength to the spirit. In all these ways those who before were sick and weak on account of their sins, now become healthy and strong by grace. O glorious and holy name, found worthy to have such power and strength!

The Fourth Feast
How the Son of God Is Sought and Adored Spiritually with the Magi by the Devout Soul

We come now to the fourth feast, the Adoration of the Magi. After the soul by God's grace has spiritually conceived, brought forth and named this dear Child, the three kings, understood here as the three powers of the soul, resolve to go in search of the Child already revealed to them in the royal city, that is, in the structure of the created universe.

The powers of the soul are rightly described as "kings," because now they rule the flesh, have dominion over the senses, and are taken up entirely, as is fitting, with the pursuit of divine things.

They seek the Child through meditation, go in search of him in heartfelt longings and inquire about him in prayerful reflections: *Where is he who has been born king of the Jews? We have seen his star in the East* [Mt 2:2]. We have seen his splendor shining in the devout mind, we have seen his radiance lighting up the inner recesses of the soul. We have heard his voice and it is soft and tender; we have tasted his sweetness and it is delightful; we have caught his fragrance and it is alluring; we have felt his embrace and it is irresistible.

Now, Herod, give us the answer, tell us where the Beloved is to be found, show us the little Child we are yearning to see. He is the one we seek and long for.

O most tender, most loving, eternal Child, you were a Babe from before the world began. When will we see you, when will we find you, when will we stand before your face? Without you, to rejoice is weariness; with you, to rejoice or weep is sheer delight. What is contrary to your will, we loathe; your good pleasure is our unending happiness. If it is such delight to weep over you, what must it be to find joy in you?

Where are you? We are looking for you. Where are you? We are searching for you in all things and above all else. Where are you who have *been born king of the Jews*, law of believers, light of the blind, leader of the poor, life of the dead, eternal salvation of all who live forever?

Scripture gives us the true answer: *In Bethlehem of Juda* [Mt 2:5]. Bethlehem means "house of bread" and Juda "one who praises."

Christ is found when we have confessed our sins and listened attentively to the teaching of the gospel, the bread of everlasting life, meditated upon it and rooted it firmly in our hearts, so that we may fulfill it by good works and proclaim it to others that they may observe it also.

We find the Child Jesus with Mary his mother when we taste the sweetness of divine contemplation, sometimes accompanied by abundant tears of consolation, after we have shed tears of sorrow and made fruitful confession of our sins. We find the Child when prayer, which at the outset saw us almost despairing, leaves us rejoicing and assured of forgiveness. How happy such a "Mary" by whom Jesus is conceived, from whom he is born, and with whom he is found in tenderness and delight.

You also, native powers of the soul, whom I have called kings, must go in search of the Child Jesus as did the three Magi, to worship him and offer him your gifts. Worship him with reverence, for he is the Creator, the Redeemer, and the Rewarder of all. Worship him as the Creator, for he fashioned our very being; as the Redeemer, for he restored life to our spirit; as the Rewarder, for he grants us eternal life.

Adore him with reverence, you kings, for he is the most powerful king; adore him with veneration, for he is the most wise teacher; adore him with gladness, for he is the most generous prince. Do not be content to adore him, offer him gifts as well. Offer him the gold of ardent love, the frankincense of devout contemplation, the myrrh of bitter sorrow. Offer him the gold of love for the graces he has bestowed on you, the frankincense of devotion, for the joys he has prepared for you, and the myrrh of sorrow for the sins you have committed. Offer gold in honor of Christ's eternal godhead, frankincense in honor of the holiness of his soul, and myrrh in honor of his bodily sufferings.

Devout soul, in this way seek the Child Jesus, adore him and offer him your gifts.

The Fifth Feast
How the Son of God Is Spiritually Presented in the Temple by a Devout Soul

In the fifth and last place, the devout soul turns to consider how this little Child is to be presented in the Temple and offered to the Lord. He came to birth in the soul by the fulfillment of divinely inspired works, he was given his name when the soul tasted heavenly sweetness, he was sought for and found, then worshipped and adored, when it offered him spiritual gifts. He is now presented in the Temple by offering him, fervently and humbly, the thanks which are his due.

This blest "Mary," the spiritual mother of Jesus, was cleansed through penance in conceiving her holy Son; she was strengthened in a number of ways by giving birth to him; she was consoled in her deepest heart by assigning him his holy name, and she was filled with the divine life by adoring him with the kings.

What then remains to be done? Only this—to carry the Son of God and Son of the Virgin Mary to the heavenly Jerusalem and into the Temple of the godhead and there present him to the Father.

Go up, then, spiritual "Mary," not now into the hill country, but to the dwelling place which is the heavenly Jerusalem, to the palace of that city which is above. There, before the throne of the eternal Trinity and undivided Unity, kneel down humbly in spirit and present your Son to God the Father, as you praise, glorify and bless the Father, Son, and Holy Spirit.

With rejoicing praise God the Father, by whose inspiration you conceived your resolve to lead a life of holiness. With reverence, glorify God the Son, by whose grace you put into effect the resolve you conceived. Bless and adore God the Holy Spirit, by whose strength you have so far remained steadfast in good works.

Devout soul, glorify God the Father for all his gifts and for all the good you do. By his mysterious inspirations, he called you away from the world, saying: *Return, return O Shulammite* [Sg 6:12]. The meaning of those words will be found in the first meditation of another little work I have written.

Magnify God the Son in all his saints. By his mysterious grace he delivered you from the devil's slavery, saying: *Take my yoke upon you* [Mt 11:29] and cast off the yoke of the devil. His yoke is bitter, mine is sweet. His will lead you to eternal torment and pain; mine will bring you to everlasting joy and *quiet resting places* [Is 32:18]. Should the devil's yoke by chance bring you some delight, it is false and passing. My yoke brings true joy and leads to eternal salvation. Sometimes the devil exalts his servants for a little while, only to put them to shame for all eternity. Everyone who honors me may suffer humiliations for a time, only to reign and be glorified forever.

This is the teaching God's Son gave you, sometimes directly himself, other times through his friends and the teachers he appointed. By that teaching, he delivered you from the wiles of the devil and the seductions of the world and the flesh.

Devout soul, always bless and honor God the Holy Spirit who strengthened you in all goodness by his gracious consolations, saying: *Come to me all who labor and are heavy laden and I will give you rest* [Mt 11:28].

Devout soul, consider how inexperienced and easily allured, how frail and weak you were. You were so much at home in worldly pleasures, besotted with earthly delights as by the dregs of wine, like pigs wallowing in filth. You were surrounded by so many and such terrible snares of the ancient enemy. On all sides you were faced by so much false advice and all kinds of obstacles and countless weapons used by relatives, friends, and others close to you to keep you from the path of love and do you harm.

How could you have persevered in doing good, shackled as you were by the chains of sin? How could you have advanced in virtue, had not the grace of the Holy Spirit mercifully come to your aid and so often graciously strengthened and refreshed you? Refer then all the good you do to him, ascribe none of it to yourself.

Utter these words with an upright and faithful intention: *O Lord, you have wrought for me all my works* [cf. Is 26:1]. In your sight I am nothing and I can do nothing. By your gift I continue to exist, and without you I am good for nothing.

To you, most compassionate *Father of mercies* [2 Cor 1:3], I offer what is yours. I commend and commit my unworthy self to you. I humbly acknowledge my ingratitude for all the gifts you have showered upon me.

To you, most blessed Father, eternal Majesty, be praise, glory, and thanksgiving. By your infinite power, you created me out of nothing.

I praise, glorify and give you thanks, most blessed Son, radiance of the Father's glory [Heb 1:3]. By your eternal wisdom you saved me from death.

I bless, sanctify, and adore you, most holy, life-giving Spirit. In your love and mercy you called me from sin to grace, from the world to a life of holiness, from exile to the fatherland, from labor to rest, and from grief to the joys of heavenly and sublime happiness.

May this be granted to us all by Jesus Christ, the Son of the Virgin Mary, who lives and reigns with the Father and the Holy Spirit forever and ever. Amen.

Christ, The One Teacher of All

Only one is your teacher, Christ. [Mt 23:10]

This text states that there is but one fontal principle of cognitive illumination; namely, Christ, *who, since he is the splendor of the Father's glory and the representation of his being, sustains all things by the word of his power*, as we read in Hebrews [1:3]. He it is who is the source of *all wisdom* according to Sirach: *The fount of wisdom is the Word of God on high* [1:1]. Christ himself is the fount of all true knowledge. Indeed, according to John: He is *the Way, and the Truth, and the Life* [14:6].

There are three degrees of true and certain knowledge according to what Hugh of Saint Victor writes in *On the Sacraments*: "There are three levels in the development of faith by which faith tends and proceeds to perfection as it increases. The first is to choose through piety; the second to approve by reason; and the third to apprehend by truth." Accordingly, it appears that there are three ways of knowing. The first is through the faith of pious assent; the second is through the approval of right reason; and the third is through the clarity of pure contemplation. The first is related to the habit of that virtue which is faith; the second to the habit of that gift which is understanding; and the third to that habit of blessedness which is purity of heart. Since there are three modes of knowledge, namely, that of faith, that of rational discourse, and that of contemplation, Christ is the principle and the cause of all of these. He is the principle of the first in as far as he is the Way; of the second in as far as he is the Truth; and of the third in as far as he is the Life.

Christ as Teacher of the Way

As the Way, Christ is the master and principle of that knowledge which is had by faith. This knowledge is twofold; namely through revelation and through authority. As Augustine writes in *On the Utility of Belief*: "What we understand, we owe to reason; what we believe, we owe to authority." There would be no authority unless it were preceded by revelation, as we read in the Second Letter of Peter: *We possess the prophetic message as something altogether reliable. Keep your attention fixed closely on it as you would on a lamp shining in a dark place* [2:19]. The authority of the prophetic word is implied in this, and then the reason is added: *Prophecy has never been forward by man's willing it. It is rather that men who were impelled by the Holy Spirit have spoken under God's influence* [1:21]. Since it is in these two ways that we are to come to the knowledge of faith, it is impossible to do so except through Christ, the Giver, who is the principle of all revelation by his coming into the mind, and the foundation of all authority by his coming into the flesh.

He comes into the mind as the revelatory light of all prophetic vision according to Daniel: *He reveals deep and hidden things and knows things determined in darkness, and the light is with him* [2:22], that is, the light of divine wisdom which is Christ. According to John: *I am the Light of the world, he who comes after me will not walk in darkness* [8:12]. John says: *Believe in the light*

while you have the light, that you may become children of the light
[12:36], because it is written: *To those who believe in his name, he
gave the power to become sons of God* [1:12]. Without this light,
which is Christ, no one can penetrate the mysteries of faith.
For this reason, it is written in Wisdom: *Send her, that is, Wisdom, from your holy heaven and from the throne of your majesty, that
she may be with me and work with me, that I may know what is accepted in your sight. For what man can know the counsel of God, and
who can think what God wills?* [9:10, 13]. From this we are given
to understand that it is impossible to arrive at the certain revelation of faith except through the coming of Christ into the
mind.

He also came into the flesh as the word of approbation for
all prophetic utterances. We read in Hebrews: *In many and diverse ways God spoke to our fathers through the prophets in times past;
in this, the final age, he has spoken to us through his Son* [1:1-2].
While Christ himself is the word of the Father, full of
power—according to Ecclesiastes: *His word is filled with power;
and no one could say to him; Why do you act in this way?* [8:4]. He is
also the word full of truth. Indeed, he is truth itself, as we read
in John: *Sanctify them in truth. Your word is truth* [17:7]. The
"Gloss" comments on this in the following way: "*In truth*
means `in me' who am truth. This is clear from the fact that
John adds *Your word is truth*; that is, `I am the truth'; in Greek,
logos, and in Latin, *verbum*." Since authority accrues to that
word which is powerful and true, and Christ as the word of the
Father is the power and wisdom of God, it follows that the
firmness of all authority is founded, stabilized, and brought to
completion in him.

All authentic scripture and all the preachers of scripture,
therefore, are related to Christ who comes into the flesh, for he
is the foundation of the entire Christian faith according to the
First Letter to the Corinthians: *According to the grace given to me,
that I might lay the foundation as a wise architect. No one can lay any
other foundation than that which has been laid, which is Christ Jesus*
[3:10-11]. He is the foundation of all authentic doctrine,
whether apostolic or prophetic according to both Laws, the

Old and the New. This is the meaning of Ephesians: *You have been built upon the foundation of the apostles and prophets; Jesus Christ himself is the supreme cornerstone* [2:20]. It is clear, therefore, that it is Christ who teaches the knowledge of faith in as far as he is the Way, and in terms of his twofold coming; namely, into the mind and into the flesh.

Christ as Teacher of the Truth

It is he who teaches rational knowledge in as far as he is the Truth. Scientific knowledge necessarily requires immutable truth on the part of the thing known and infallible certitude on the part of the knower. Whatever is known, indeed, is necessary in itself and certain to the knower. We know as Aristotle says, "when we judge the reason why a thing is, and we know that it is impossible for it to be otherwise."

On the part of that which can be known, immutable truth is required. Such a truth cannot be a created truth simply and absolutely, since every creature is capable of motion and change. It is, rather, the truth which creates that is fully immutable. Thus it is written in the Psalms: *In the beginning, O Lord, you established the earth, and the heavens are the work of your hands. They shall perish, but you will remain though all of them grow old like a garment. You change them like clothing, and they are changed. But you are the same, and your years have no end* [102:26-28]. The apostle writes in Hebrews, this is addressed to the Son of God, who is the word, the art, and the reason of the all-powerful God [cf. 1:10]. He is, therefore, the sempiternal truth according to the psalm: *Your word remains forever, O Lord, and your truth for eternity* [119:89]. While things have being in themselves, they also have being in the mind and in the eternal reason as well. They are not entirely immutable in the first and second modes of being, but only in the third; namely, in as far as they are in the eternal Word. It follows, therefore, that nothing can render things perfectly knowable unless Christ is present, the Son of God, and the Teacher.

Augustine writes in *On Free Will*: "Do not deny in any way that there is unchangeable truth, containing those things which are immutably true, which I cannot say is yours or mine or any man's, but which presents itself commonly to all who perceive the eternal truths." The same thing is said in *On the Trinity*. When impious people see the rules according to which each ought to live, "where do they see them? Not, indeed, in their own nature, since without doubt these things are to be seen by the mind, and their minds are admittedly mutable. But these rules are seen as unchangeable by anyone who can see them at all. Nor can the answer be found in the state of their own mind, since these rules are rules of righteousness, and their minds are admittedly unrighteous. Where, then, are those rules written wherein even the unrighteous man knows and recognizes what is righteous, and wherein he knows that he should possess something that he does not possess? Where are they written except in that book of light which is called Truth, wherein every just law is transcribed, and from which justice is transferred to the heart of man not by migrating to it, but by being impressed upon it?" This is stated also in *On True Religion*, *Concerning Music*, and in *The Retractions*.

Secondly, on the part of the knower, this kind of knowledge requires certitude. Certitude can be had neither from a principle that can be deceived nor from a light that can be obscured. The necessary light is not that of the created intelligence but that of uncreated Wisdom which is Christ. It is written in Wisdom: *God gave me true knowledge of existing things, that I might know the organization of the universe and the power of its elements, the beginning and the end, and the mid-point of times* [7:17-18]. And later it says: *Wisdom, the artificer of all, taught me* [7:22]. Then the writer adds the reason for this: *She is an aura of the might of God and a pure effusion of the glory of the Almighty; therefore nothing that is sullied enters into her. For she is the refulgence of eternal light, the spotless mirror of the power of God. . . . For she is fairer than the sun and surpasses every constellation of the stars. Compared to light, she takes precedence. . . . She reaches from end to end mightily and governs all things well* [7:25-26; 8:1]. Because of this, John writes: *He was the true light that enlightens every one* [1:9], and the "Gloss" comments: "That light is not the true one which gives light from another source and not from itself."

Of itself the light of the created intellect is not sufficient for the certain comprehension of anything without the light of the eternal Word. For this reason, Augustine writes in the *Soliloquies*: "In this sun three things may be discerned: that it is; that it shines; and that it illumines. There are also three things in the most secret depth of God: that he is; that he knows; and that he makes it possible for other things to be known." A little before this he says that "as the earth cannot be seen except by means of a light that illumines it, likewise, those things which are taught in the various disciplines are of such a sort that, without doubt, anyone can concede that they can be understood as most true, even though we must believe that they are intelligible only if they are illumined by something else as by their own sun." Again, in *On the Trinity*, Augustine tells us of the boy who, without benefit of a teacher, responded correctly to certain questions about geometry, and he rejects the position of Plato, who held that souls were infused with knowledge prior to their existence in the body. According to Augustine, this is not true. "Rather," he says, "we ought to believe that the nature of the intellectual mind is formed in such a way that, by being naturally subject to intelligible realities according to the arrangement of the Creator, it sees these truths in a certain incorporeal light of a unique kind, just as the eye of the body sees things all around it in this corporeal light. It is created with a capacity for this light and is adapted to it." What this light might be is described in *On Free Will*: "That beauty of truth and wisdom which does not pass with time nor move from place to place. It is neither interrupted by night nor shut off by shadows, nor is it subject to the bodily senses. To all those from the entire world who love it and turn to it, it is near, everlasting for all. It is in no place yet is absent nowhere. It admonishes from without and teaches within. No one judges it, and without it no one can judge well. Thus, it is manifest to our minds as something that is without doubt greater than our minds, since by it alone each mind is made wise and judges not concerning it, but through it concerning other things." We find the same things in *On True Religion*, *On the Trinity* as well as in *On the Teacher*, where throughout the entire work, he proves the conclusion that our teacher is one: namely, Christ.

Christ as Teacher of the Life

Finally, in as far as Christ is the Life, he is the master of contemplative knowledge. With this the soul is concerned in two ways that correspond to two types of nourishment; namely, the inner nourishment in the Godhead, and the external nourishment in the humanity. There are, therefore, two modes of contemplation; namely, a going-in and a going-out. No one can arrive at this except through Christ. He himself says in John: *I am the gate; whoever enters through me will be saved. He will go in and out and find pasture* [10:9].

The going-in is to go to Christ as the uncreated Word and the food of angels, of whom it is said in John: *In the beginning was the Word* [1:1]. Concerning this going-in it is written in another translation of the psalm: *I will go in to the place of the wonderful tabernacle, up to the dwelling place of God, with a cry of joy and praise and festive sound* [42:5]. This refers to the heavenly Jerusalem. No one can enter into the contemplation of it unless led in through the uncreated Word which is Christ. Therefore Dionysius writes in *On the Angelic Hierarchy*: "By calling on Jesus, the light of the Father, who is the true light that enlightens every man coming into the world, we have access to the principal light: namely, the Father. In as far as possible, we look to the illumination of the most sacred words given by the Father. In as far as we are able, we will consider the hierarchies of the heavenly spirits manifest in them for us symbolically and anagogically, looking to the principal and super-principal divine clarity of the Father by means of the immaterial and steadfast eyes of the mind."

The going-out is to the incarnate Word, the milk of infants about whom we read in John: *The Word was made flesh and dwelt among us* [1:14]. The Song of Songs speaks of this going-out: *Come forth, daughter of Sion, and see King Solomon in the crown with which his mother crowned him on the day of his marriage, and on the day of the joy of his heart* [3:11]. The crown with which the true peacemaker, Solomon, was crowned by his mother is the immaculate flesh, which he assumed of the Virgin Mary. It is called the marriage crown because through it he espoused to himself the holy Mother Church, which was formed from his side as Eve was formed from the side of the man. Through that flesh the entire ecclesiastical hierarchy is purged, illuminated, and perfected. It is to be looked upon as the life-giving nourishment of the entire Church according to John: *My flesh is food indeed; and my blood is drink indeed*. For this reason, the text continues, *He who eats my flesh and drinks my blood has eternal life* [6:56-58].

In the book *On the Soul and Spirit* we read: "The life of the soul is twofold; one life by which it lives in the flesh, and another by which it lives in God. Indeed, a person has two senses; the one interior and the other exterior. Each of these has its own good in which it delights; the interior sense in the contemplation of the divinity and the exterior sense in the contemplation of the humanity. For this reason, God became flesh in order to beatify the whole person in himself, so that whether `he goes in' or `goes out' he will `find pasture' in his maker; pasture without in the flesh of the Savior, and pasture within in the divinity of the Creator." This going-in to the divinity and going-out to the humanity is nothing other than the "ascent to heaven" and the "descent to earth," which is accomplished through Christ as through the ladder mentioned in Genesis: *In his dream Jacob saw a ladder standing on the earth, with its top touching heaven; and he saw angels ascending and descending on it* [28:12]. The ladder symbolized Christ; the ascending and descending of the angels symbolizes the illumination of contemplatives, who are ascending and descending, thus indicating the two modes of contemplation carried out by the interior and exterior reading of the book written within and without. This is the book mentioned in the Book of Revelations: *In the right hand of the one sitting on the throne I saw a book written within and without, and sealed with seven seals*. It goes on to say that *no one in heaven or on earth or under the earth could open the book or examine its contents* [5:3]. To this it adds that, *the Lion of the tribe of Judah, by his victory, has won the right to open the book and to break its seven seals* [5:5].

If, therefore, the person who opened the book and broke its seals deserves to be called Teacher, then the title certainly belongs to Christ; for he is the "lion that rose up" and the "lamb that was slain." It is then apparent that in all the different kinds of knowledge "our Teacher is one," namely, Christ, because he is the Way, the Truth, and the Life.

From the foregoing, it is clear by what order and by which author we are to arrive at wisdom. The order is this: that we begin with the firmness of faith and proceed through the serenity of reason so as to arrive at the sweetness of contemplation. This is the order implied by Christ when he said: *I am the Way, the Truth, and the Life* [Jn 14:6]. In this way we can see the fulfillment of what is written in Proverbs: *The path of the just is like a shining light and it increases in brilliance until the perfect day* [4:18]. The Saints held to this order, listening to Isaiah, according to another translation: "Unless you believe, you will not understand." Philosophers who neglected faith and based their thought totally on reason were ignorant of this order and could in no way arrive at contemplation. Augustine says in *On the Trinity*: "The eye of the human mind, since it is weak, is dazzled in the presence of such excellent light unless it is purged through the justice of faith."

Exemplarism and Knowledge

It is clear who the model and teacher is. For Christ, who directs and aids our understanding, does so not only in a general sense, as is true with all the works of nature, and not only in a special sense, as in the works of grace and meritorious virtue, but he directs and aids us in a certain middle way between these two. To understand this, we must note that in creatures there are three levels of conformity to God. Some things are conformed to God as vestige, some as image, and some as similitude. A vestige is related to God as to the creative principle. An image is related to God not only as to a principle but also as to its motivating object, as Augustine writes in *On the Trinity*: "The soul is an image of God in that it is capable of God and of participation in the divine life," namely, through knowledge and love. The similitude is related to God not only as to principle and object, but also as to a gift infused into it.

In those creaturely operations which proceed from the creature itself, in as far as it is a vestige—and this is universally the case with natural actions—God cooperates as principle and cause. In those actions which proceed from the creature as an image—and such are the intellectual actions by which the soul sees immutable truth itself—God cooperates as object and as motivating reason. In those actions which proceed from a creature, in as far as it is a similitude—and such are meritorious actions—God cooperates as a gift infused through grace. Augustine says in *On the City of God*: "God is the cause of all being, the principle of all knowing, and the order of all living."

The meaning of the term "principle of knowledge" must be understood in a sound way. It does not mean that God is the only, or bare, or total means of knowledge. If he were the only ground of knowledge, there would be no difference between the knowledge of science and that of wisdom; nor would there be any difference between knowledge in the Word and knowledge of a thing in its own right. Furthermore, if he were the bare and open ground of knowledge, there would be no difference between our knowledge in this life and our knowledge in heaven. But this is clearly false, since in heaven our knowledge will be face-to-face while on earth we see *darkly and through a mirror* [1 Cor 13:12], because in this life our knowledge depends on the sense phantasms. Finally, if he were the total ground, we would have no need of species and reception to know things. This we see to be manifestly false, because when we lose one of our senses, we necessarily lose one type of knowledge. Even though Augustine considers the soul to be in contact with the eternal laws, because in some way it attains to that light at the apex of the agent intellect and the superior part of reason, yet what the philosopher says is true beyond doubt, namely, that knowledge is generated in us by way of sense, memory, and experience from which the universal is formed in us. The universal is the principle of art and science. Because Plato related all certain knowledge to the intelligible or ideal world, he was justly criticized by Aristotle. Not because he was wrong in affirming the ideas and the eternal reasons, since Augustine praises him for this, but because—despising the sensible world—he wishes to reduce all certain knowledge to the ideas. In doing this, he would seem to provide a firm basis for the way of wisdom which proceeds according to the eternal reasons, but he destroyed the way of science which proceeds according to created reasons. On the other hand, Aristotle provided a firm foundation for the way of science while neglecting the way of wisdom. It seems, therefore, that among the philosophers, the word of wisdom is to be granted to Plato and the word of science to Aristotle. For the former looked above all at the higher realities, while the latter looked principally to the lower things.

Both the word of science and that of wisdom were given by the Holy Spirit to Augustine as an outstanding expositor of the whole of scripture, and it is clear from his writings that he carried this out in a pre-eminent way. To an even greater degree, this is true of Paul and Moses; in the one as in a minister of the law of figures, in the other as in a minister of the law of grace. Acts says of Moses that he was *educated in all the wisdom of the Egyptians* [7:22], and again it was said to him on the mountain, *See that you make them according to the pattern shown to you on the mountain* [Ex 25:40]. In the case of Paul, he himself said that among the simple he would not show himself as knowing anything but Christ Jesus and him crucified. According to the First Letter to the Corinthians, however, he spoke wisdom among the perfect; a wisdom he himself had learned when he was taken up to the third heaven according to the Second Letter to the Corinthians. This was realized in the highest degree in our Lord Jesus Christ, who was the principal Law-giver. At one and the same time, he was perfectly a man in history and yet in possession of the goal. He alone, therefore, is the principal teacher.

Respectful Dialogue with Christ, the Teacher

As principal teacher, therefore, it is he above all who is to be honored, listened to, and questioned. He is to be honored above all others, since he attributes the dignity of master to himself. According to Matthew: *Do not be called Rabbi, for one is your Master, and you are all brothers* [23:8]. He wished to reserve the dignity of master to himself according to John: *You call me Lord and Master; and you do well, for so I am* [13:13]. He is to be honored not only by word of mouth but also in reality through imitation. For this reason the text adds: *If I have washed your feet, I who am Teacher and Lord, then you must wash each others' feet* [13:14], because we read in Luke: *He who does not follow me cannot be my disciple* [14:27].

We must listen to him above all others through the humility of faith, according to Isaiah: *The Lord has given me a well-trained tongue that I might know how to sustain the weary with my word. Morning after morning he opens my ear that I might hear him as my master* [50:4]. Twice it says *he opens,* because it is not sufficient that our ear be opened to understand unless it is opened also to obey. We read, therefore, in Matthew: *He who has ears to hear, let him hear* [13:43]. Christ teaches us not only in word but also in example. Therefore, he who hears does not hear perfectly unless he brings understanding to the words and obedience to the deeds. This is the meaning of Luke: *Everyone will be perfect if he becomes like his master* [6:40].

Finally, we must ask him questions out of the desire to learn and not in order to test him as do curious and unbelieving people. We read about this in Matthew: *Some of the scribes answered saying, "Master, we wish to see a sign from you"* [12:38]. They had seen signs over and over again, and yet they ask for still another. This shows that human curiosity has no limit and does not deserve to be led to truth. This explains why he answered them that no sign would be given them except the sign of Jonas, the prophet. Jesus is not to be interrogated in this way but rather with desire as Nicodemus inquired of him. John tells us that: *He came to Jesus by night and said to him: Rabbi, we know that you have come from God as our Master,* etc. [3:2]. The text then goes on to say that Jesus opened to him the mysteries of faith, because he did not ask for signs of power but for examples of truth.

We are to ask this teacher about those matters that pertain to science, discipline, and goodness. A psalm says: *Teach me goodness and discipline and science* [119:66]. Science consists in the knowledge of truth; discipline consists in avoiding evil; goodness consists in choosing the good. The first concerns truth; the second holiness; the third charity. We ought to ask him about those matters that pertain to the truth of science, but not with the desire to test him as the disciples of the Pharisees tested him. It is written in Matthew: *Master, we know that you are truthful,* etc. [22:16]. Since their question arose from an evil intention, he replied, *Why do you tempt me, you hypocrites?* [Mt 22:18]. But because the question itself was good, he gave a true answer: *Render therefore to Caesar the things that are Caesar's and to God the things that are God's* [Mt 22:21].

Secondly, we should ask him about those things that pertain to the discipline of sanctity as did the young man in Mark: *Good Master, what shall I do that I might possess eternal life?* [10:17]. He answered that he should keep the commandments, and that if he wished to be perfect he should observe the counsels, for in these is found the perfect discipline of morals and an aid against those things that incline us to sin. We should ask him also about those things that pertain to the kindness of love, following the example of the doctor of the Law in Matthew: *Master, which is the greatest commandment of the*

Law? He said to him: *You shall love the Lord your God with your whole heart and mind and soul. This is the greatest and first commandment. And the second is like it: You shall love your neighbor as yourself* [22:36-39]. In this we see that the *fullness of the law is love* [Rom 13:10].

It is about these three things that we should question Christ, our teacher; for the entire law of Christ is related to them. All the teaching of the ministerial doctor should be concerned with these three matters, so that the office of teaching might be carried out in a fitting manner under the supreme Master. Every master who carries out the office of teaching should seek to understand the truth of faith according to the First Letter to Timothy: *I speak the truth and I do not lie, the teacher of the nations in faith and truth* [2:7]. It is written in the Second Letter to Peter: *It was not by way of cleverly concocted myths that we taught you about the coming in power of our Lord Jesus Christ, for we are eyewitnesses of his power* [1:16].

He should also seek the discipline of sanctity of soul according to the Second Letter to Timothy: *I, Paul, have been appointed preacher and apostle in the service of the gospel, and for this reason I suffer these things* [1:11-12], because, according to Proverbs: *Learning comes to man through patience* [19:11]. As it is not fitting that the foolish should teach wisdom, neither is it fitting that the impatient should teach patience, nor that the undisciplined should teach discipline. In matters of moral behavior, examples move more strongly than words.

He should seek the kindness of the love of God and neighbor. Ecclesiastes writes: *The sayings of the wise are like goads, like spikes fixed on high, which through the advice of teachers are given out by one pastor* [12:11]. I tell you, these words are the words of divine love, and they penetrate to the depths of the heart. These words are said to be given through the counsel of teachers by one pastor. While divine love is praised and recommended in many words in the writings of both the Testaments, yet it is but one Word alone that inspires, and he indeed is both pasture and pastor of all. All those words came from the same one and tend toward the same one. For this reason, they are expressly said to be given through the counsel of teachers, all of whom mean the same thing. Since all the doctors of the Christian law ought to seek the bond of charity, they ought also to agree in their thinking. It is written in James: *Not many of you, brothers, should wish to become teachers* [3:1]. This is said not to prohibit us from communicating the gift of knowledge, since Moses says in Numbers: *Would that he would grant that all the people were prophets, and that the Lord would grant them his Spirit* [11:29]. And the First Letter of Peter says: *Put your gifts at the service of one another, each one as he has received grace* [4:10]. This means that they should not have diverse and deceptive opinions, but all should teach the same thing as we read in the First Letter to the Corinthians: *I beg you, brothers, in the name of our Lord Jesus Christ, to agree in what you say; let there be no factions among you; rather be united in one mind and one judgment* [1:10].

For dissenting opinions arise from presumption according to Proverbs: *Among the proud there is always discord* [13:10] and *it begets confusion* according to the First Letter to Timothy: *Whoever teaches in any other way not holding to the sound doctrine of our Lord Jesus Christ and the teaching proper to true religion is proud and ignorant, and is a man sick in his passion for polemics and controversy. From these come envy, dissensions, blasphemy, evil suspicions, and conflicts of men with twisted minds who have lost the sense of truth* [6:3-5].

These three are the things that impede the perception of truth, namely, presumption on the part of the senses, dissent of opinions, and the despair of finding truth. In opposition to these Christ says: "Only one is your teacher, Christ." Christ says that he is our teacher, so that we might not be presumptuous about our knowledge. He says that our teacher is one with whom we might not fall into disagreement. He says that he is your teacher, because he is ready to assist us lest we give in to despair. Above all, he has the desire to help us. He has the knowledge necessary, and he can teach us by sending that Spirit of whom he speaks in John 16:13: *When he comes, the Spirit of truth, he will teach you all truth* [16:13].

May Jesus Christ, the Son of the most blessed Mary, deign to come to our aid. Amen.

Christ, God's Word and Mediator of the Holy Spirit

Prayer directed to the Holy Spirit was a rarity in the Middle Ages. Theologians such as Bonaventure echoed the ancient tradition, which considered the Holy Spirit a gift to be requested in prayer. The seven gifts of the Holy Spirit, fear, piety, knowledge, fortitude, counsel, knowledge and wisdom, were contained in the one unique gift of the Holy Spirit given by the Father and the Son. The following prayer for the gifts of the Holy Spirit serves as the conclusion to *The Tree of Life*. Similar to *The Five Feasts of the Child Jesus*, *The Tree of Life* is a meditation on gospel events intended to foster a profound spiritual transformation in Christ, the Word of God. It is fitting that Bonaventure invites readers to turn to Christ in prayer after encouraging them to consider his life, death, and resurrection. As the Word made flesh and eternally present with the Father and the Holy Spirit, Christ mediates the Holy Spirit to those who call out to him in prayer.

Prayer for the Gifts of the Holy Spirit

We pray, therefore, to the most clement Father through you, his only-begotten Son, who became man for us, was crucified and glorified, so that from his treasures he may send into us the Spirit of sevenfold grace, who *rested* upon you in all fullness: the spirit, I say, of *wisdom* so we may taste the life-giving flavors of the fruit of the tree of life, which truly you are; also the gift of *understanding*, whereby the contuitions of our mind may be illuminated; the gift of *counsel*, whereby we may follow your footsteps along the correct paths; the gift of *fortitude*, whereby we may be able to weaken the violence of the attacking enemies; the gift of *knowledge*, whereby we may be filled with the lights of your sacred doctrine to distinguish good and evil; the gift of *piety*, whereby we may receive a merciful heart; the gift of *fear*, whereby, drawing back from every evil, we may be calmed by reverential consideration of your eternal Majesty. You wished that we ask for these things in that sacred prayer which you taught us; and now we ask to obtain these things to the praise of your most holy name, to which with the Father and the Holy Spirit, be all honor and glory, thanksgiving, splendor, and authority for ever and ever. Amen.

Glossary of Terms

Contuition

The greatest knowledge of God, albeit indirect, which the intellect can acquire. In the systematic consideration of divine truth, the gift of understanding purifies the heart, thereby preparing the intellect for the contuition of God. As the intellect considers the vestiges of material creatures and the images and similitudes of rational creatures, it ascends to the knowledge of the Trinity. When the intellect arrives at this point in contemplation, it can go no further; instead, it is called to rest from all speculative labor and entrust itself to God. A deeper knowledge of the divine is possible only through the gift of charity by which the soul is united with the Trinity.

Emanation

A fundamental principle of reality whereby all that exists comes from God and ultimately returns to God. The natural world mirrors this truth when rain falls from the clouds only to return through evaporation. Salvation history reveals a similar dynamic when the Christ, the Son of God, comes forth from the Father in the incarnation and returns to the Father in the ascension. The inner life of the Trinity is the model of every expression of emanation, since it is the Son and Spirit who come forth from the Father and return to the Father in the eternal, impenetrable mystery of the Godhead.

Exemplarity

A fundamental principle of reality whereby all that exists is patterned after the divine and exemplifies a degree of similarity with the divine. The eternal exemplar is the Son who, as the Uncreated Word, is the perfect expression of the Father. Creatures derive their perfection from the eternal exemplar according to their participation in the goodness of God. The Son is the exemplar of creation, because all things were created through him and, together with him, are called to return to the Father. As the Incarnate Word, the Son is the temporal exemplar and mirror of all graces, virtues, and merits. The perfection of the incarnate Word is seen in the Church in accord with the state and the respective gifts of the individual members. Just as creatures do not reflect the total perfection of the eternal exemplar, members of the Church do not reflect the total perfection of the temporal exemplar. The members reflect, however, the perfection of the incarnate Word according to the degree they imitate his example of holiness.

Gloss

An authoritative compilation of patristic and medieval interpretations of selected scriptural terms and texts.

Literal, Allegorical, Moral, Anagogical Meaning

Different levels of meaning which are uncovered in the sacred scripture in the process of interpretation. The literal meaning or sense is usually readily apparent and serves as the basis for further study. Scriptural language often evokes images related to faith, hence an allegorical sense is embedded in the text. The moral or tropological sense is apparent in the ethical imperatives derived from scriptural passages. The anagogical or mystical meaning refers to the hope for eternal life that the sacred scriptures engender.

Macrocosm and Microcosm

A system of classification and comparison in which the cosmos or universe is the macrocosm while the human being is the microcosm. The macrocosm was created for the sake of the microcosm, and the two correspond to each other. The ages of the world have a direct counterpart to the ages of human history, and the elements of the cosmos have a direct counterpart in the elements which constitute the human being.

Material, Formal, Final, Efficient Cause

The Aristotelian theory of causality used to highlight the various components of a literary work . The material cause refers to the material or literary sources used by the author. The formal cause is the structure or pattern given by the author to the material. The purpose behind the decision to write is the final cause, while the efficient cause is the author responsible for writing the literary text.

Powers of the Soul

The rational part of the soul is understood in terms of the rational, concupiscible, and irascible powers. The rational power has the capacity to discern truth and is linked with the theological virtue of faith. The concupiscible power has the capacity to enkindle the desire for the good and is linked to the theological virtue of charity. The irascible power has the capacity to endure evil and is linked to the theological virtue of hope.

Principle of Knowledge

Theory of knowledge, based on Augustine's teaching on illumination, describing how human beings come to know sense objects with certainty. Knowledge is dependent upon the infused light of God, which works together with the innate light of human reason. Certain apprehension and judgment of sense objects, which are mutable and transitory by nature, would be impossible without the assurance of universal and eternal standards afforded by divine illumination.

Topical Inferential Rule

A rule of logic used in dialectical arguments to deduce conclusions from inference.

Vestige, Image, Similitude

Analogical relationship of creatures to the trinitarian God. Vestiges of the divine are those creatures who in a distant yet distinct fashion mirror the power, wisdom, and goodness of the triune God. Angels and human being are images of the divine, because they possess the trinitarian powers of memory, intelligence, and will. As images of God, these rational creatures reflect the divine in a close and distinct manner. Similitudes are rational creatures who reveal the closest similarity to God. This highest degree of trinitarian likeness is manifested in souls transformed by the theological virtues of faith, hope and love.

Chronology

This chronology is based on the "Chronologia sancti bonaventurae" in *De vita, mente, fontibus et operibus s. bonaventurae*. Vol. 2 of S. Bonaventura 1274-1974, Assisi, Tipografia portiuncula, 1973, 11-14; Jacques Bougerol, *Introduction to the Works of Bonaventure*, trans. José de Vinck, Paterson, N.J., Saint Anthony's Guild Press, 1964, 171-177; and Jacques Bougerol, *Introduzione generale a san bonaventura*, 9-14, Roma, Città Nuova Editrice, 1990.

1217   Bonaventure is born, the son of Giovanni of Fidanza and Maria di Ritello, in the small city of Bagnoregio, not far from Orvietto in central Italy.

1225-35   As a young child, he is given over to the friars minor to be educated in their convent in Bagnoregio.

1226   Miraculously healed after his mother prays to Saint Francis of Assisi for his intercession.

1235-43   Studies with the Faculty of Arts at the University of Paris and concludes with the Master of Arts title.

1243   Enters into the Franciscan Order and is affiliated with the Roman province of friars.

1243-48   Studies theology under the guidance of the Franciscan masters Alexander of Hales, John of La Rochelle, Odo Rigaldi, and William of Middleton.

1248-50   As a Bachelor of Sacred Scripture works on *The Commentary on John*, *The Commentary on Ecclesiastes*, and *The Commentary on Luke*.

1250-52   As a Bachelor of Sentences, undertakes an exposition of the *Sentences* of Peter Lombard, which eventually forms a four-volume *Commentary on the Sentences*.

1252-53   Preaches and participates in theological disputations at the University of Paris. As a full Bachelor of Theology, he produces *The Disputed Questions on the Knowledge of Christ, The Disputed Questions on the Trinity*, and *The Disputed Questions on Evangelical Perfection*.

1253-54   Passes examination and is recognized by the chancellor of the University of Paris as a Master of Theology with the license to teach theology.

1254-57   Holds the position of Master of Theology in the School of the Friars Minor at the University of Paris. Comments on the sacred scriptures, preaches, and determines disputed questions of theology.

1257   Elected Minister General of the Order of Friars Minor in the presence of Pope Alexander IV at the General Chapter held in Rome on February 2. Marks his acceptance as a Master of Theology by the faculty at the University of Paris with the sermon *Christ, the One Teacher*.

1257-73   Travels extensively throughout Europe as Minister General. Numerous sermons and writings, including *The Journey of the Soul into God, The Major and Minor Lives of Saint Francis, The Triple Way, The Tree of Life*, and *The Five Feasts of the Child Jesus*, originate in this period of intense pastoral activity.

1273   Named as Bishop of Albano by Pope Gregory X on May 28. Consecrated as Bishop of Albano on November 11 or 12.

1274   Attends the Council of Lyon where he works to reconcile the Greek and Latin Churches. Dies on July 15 and is buried in the church of the friars minor in Lyon.

1482   Canonized by Pope Sixtus IV on April 14.

1587   Declared Doctor of the Church by Pope Sixtus V on March 14.

Select Bibliography

Critical Editions of Saint Bonaventure's Writings

Doctoris Seraphici S. Bonaventurae Opera Omnia. Ed. PP. Collegii a S. Bonaventura. 10 vols. Quaracchi: Collegium S. Bonaventurae, 1882-1902.

Sancti bonaventurae sermones dominicales. Ed. Jacques Guy Bougerol. Grottaferrata: Collegio S. Bonaventura, 1977.

Studies on Saint Bonaventure's Life and Writings

Bougerol, Jacques Guy. *Introduction to the Works of Bonaventure.* Trans. José de Vinck. Paterson, N.J.: St. Anthony Guild Press, 1964.

Bougerol, Jacques *Introduzione generale alle opere di san bonaventura* Roma: Città Nuova Editrice, 1990.

Corvino Francesco, *Bonaventura da Bagnoregio: francescano e pensatore.* Bari: Dedaldo Libri, 1980.

Cousins, Ewert H. *Bonaventure and the Coincidence of Opposites.* Chicago: Franciscan Herald Press, 1978.

Distelbrink, Balduinus. *Bonaventurae scripta, authentica dubia vel spuria critice recensita.* Roma: Istituto Storico Cappuccini, 1975.

Gerken, Alexander. *Theologie des Wortes. Das Verhältnis von Schöpfung und Inkarnation bei Bonaventura.* Düsseldorf: Patmos Verlag, 1963.

Gilson, Etienne. *The Philosophy of St. Bonaventure.* Trans. Dom Illtyd Trethowan and Frank J. Sheed. Paterson, N.J.: St. Anthony Guild Press, 1965.

Hayes, Zachary. *The Hidden Center. Spirituality and Speculative Christology in St. Bonaventure.* New York: Paulist Press, 1981.

Johnson, Timothy J. *Iste Pauper Clamavit. St. Bonaventure's Mendicant Theology of Prayer.* New York: Peter Lang Verlag, 1990.

Monti, Dominic. "Bonaventure's Use of 'The Divine Word' in Academic Theology" in *That Others May Know and Love. Essays in Honor of Zachary Hayes, OFM.* Ed. Michael Cusato and Edward Coughlin. St. Bonaventure, N.Y.: The Franciscan Institue, 1997, 65-88.

Nguyen Van Si, Ambrosio. *Seguire e imitare Cristo secondo san Bonaventura* Trans. Simpliciano Olgiati. Milano: Edizioni Biblioteca Francescana, 1995.

Prentice, Robert. *The Psychology of Love according to St. Bonaventure.* St. Bonaventure, N.Y.: The Franciscan Institute, 1951.

Ratzinger, Joseph. *The Theology of History in St. Bonaventure.* Trans. Zachary Hayes. Chicago: Franciscan Herald Press, 1971.

Rauch, Winthir. *Das Buch Gottes. Eine systematische Untersuchung des Buchbegriffes bei Bonaventura.* München: Max Hueber Verlag, 1961.

Reist, Thomas. *Saint Bonaventure as Biblical Commentator.* Lanham, Md.: University Press of America, 1985.

Schlosser, Marianne. *Cognitio et amor: Zum kognitiven und voluntativen Grund der Gotteserfahrung nach Bonaventura.* Paderborn: Ferdinand Schöningh, 1990.

Spargo, Emma Jane Marie. *The Category of the Aesthetic in the Philosophy of Saint Bonaventure.* St. Bonaventure, N. Y.: The Franciscan Institute, 1953.

Tavard, George H. *The Forthbringer of God: Saint Bonaventure on the Virgin Mary.* Chicago: Franciscan Herald Press, 1989.

Tavard, George H. *Transiency and Permanence. The Nature of Theology According to St. Bonaventure.* Louvain: The Franciscan Institute, 1954.